Self-Regulation & Mindfulness

Over 82 Exercises & Worksheets for Sensory Processing Disorder, ADHD & Autism Spectrum Disorder

By
Varleisha Gibbs, PhD, OTD, OTR/L

Published by:
PESI Publishing & Media
PESI, Inc.
3839 White Ave.
Eau Claire, WI 54703

Cover Design: Amy Rubenzer
Editing: Blair Davis
Layout: Amy Rubenzer & Bookmasters
Photography: Arnelle Hughes

Printed in the United States of America
ISBN: 9781683730620

PESI
Publishing
& Media
www.pesipublishing.com

About The Author

Varleisha D. Gibbs, PhD, OTD, OTR/L, founded Universal Progressive Therapy, Inc. located in New Jersey. The company is focused to provide interdisciplinary and quality therapeutic services to families. As former owner of the company, she had several opportunities to provide education, treatment, and study the areas of sensory integration, Autism Spectrum disorders, as well as family-centered care. She focused her doctoral studies on family-centered care, Autism Spectrum disorders, and the use of telerehabilitation. This innovative topic led to a publication, "Family-Centered Occupational Therapy and Telerehabilitation for Children with Autism Spectrum Disorders" found in the journal of *Occupational Therapy in Healthcare*.

Dr. Gibbs speaks nationally on sensory processing strategies and self-regulation throughout the country. She is passionate to provide individuals and families with strategies to understand and care for their children. She is a full time chair/director, and associate professor, in the Master's of Occupational Therapy at Wesley College. This is Delaware's first professional degree-granting program in OT.

Contents

Introduction

As an occupational therapist, a large part of my career has been operating a private practice clinic working with children and families challenged by sensory processing disorders, attention deficit hyperactivity disorder, autism spectrum disorder and various other neurodevelopmental disorders. Many of these children came to my practice without a diagnosis, or a diagnosis without any hope for help.

Through my work with these children, I got a glimpse into their perplexing and misunderstood world. I became utterly aware that my previous education and clinical training didn't provide me with the necessary knowledge or skills to effectively treat these kids. I had to figure out how to provide the best service to these families in desperate need.

Inspired by my personal experience with meditation, compassion and psychology, I knew there had to be a better approach to treating children who have trouble self-regulating, staying focused, managing their senses, and the other challenges they experience. I also began to study neuroscience which dramatically changed my approach.

Ultimately, I wanted to enhance each child's success at home and school through utilizing the child's senses, emotions, and executive functioning skills. I began to investigate each family and their needs individually and learned how to effectively combine and implement my training and experiences. That's how I developed the integrated strategy of **Self-Regulation and Mindfulness.**

HOW TO USE THIS BOOK

This book consists of two parts:

- **Part 1** begins with an introduction to the nervous system, the brain, and the foundational science behind Self-Regulation and Mindfulness. Following are interactive lessons and worksheets appropriate for school-age children to teach them the basic internal and external structures of the brain, as well as right and left brain functions.

  - If you are looking for further knowledge or background information, "Brain Nuggets" are offered throughout part 1 to identify more technical and scientific terminology.
- **Part 2** is designed for children to learn through hands-on activities, such as self-assessments, coloring pages, games, journals and log charts. The tools are easily implemented and provide strategies for improved function at school and home leading to more daily success.

While it's science driven, the activities inside *Self-Regulation & Mindfulness* provide practical, child-friendly lessons to teach parents, educators, therapists and children about their brain and body. Therapists, teachers and parents can utilize the included tools to improve self-regulation and awareness through the following principles.

4 Self-Regulation & Mindfulness Principles

1. Multisensory Integration
2. Emotional Regulation
3. Executive Functioning
4. Mindfulness

Self-Regulation & Mindfulness defines **nine daily activity targets** that are based on useful strategies to implement the four principles in the child's daily life.

9 Daily Activity Targets
1. Touch and Heavy Work
2. Hydration and Oral Motor
3. Metronome, Timing and Sequencing Activities
4. Right and Left Brain Integration
5. Patterns and Repetition
6. Breathing and Valsalva
7. Vision and Sound
8. Movement
9. Inhibition Strategies

The focus of these activities is to implement the nine daily targets to address various levels of need for each client. Based on Maslow's hierarchy, sensory processing and mindfulness theories, I created the **Self-Regulation and Mindfulness 7-Level Hierarchy.**

The model provides a guide for exploring and understanding how to fulfill each client's needs. Sensory processing and basic biological needs are always viewed as a motivation or deficiency, regardless of the person's general level of functioning. The bottom of the pyramid represents the foundation of Safety and Preservation and describes each of the seven levels through Reciprocal Mindfulness at the top. When selecting activities for the child, you should have an idea of their general level of functioning as it relates to this hierarchy, as well as using the pyramid to set development goals and acknowledging progress. When assessing remember, Levels 1 through 4 on the hierarchy correspond with higher-level activities, Level 5 corresponds with mid-level activities, and Levels 6 and 7 correspond with foundational-level activities.

SELF-REGULATION AND MINDFULNESS 7-LEVEL HIERARCHY

What Level is the child at?

For all levels, there is an underlying acknowledgement of sensory and biological processing needed for eating, drinking, interoception, respiration, temperature, sleeping, digestion, and arousal regulation.

The higher the level, the less challenges revealed in those areas. Some children may have difficulty moving up the hierarchy and not reach the highest levels. Yet, every child has the potential to make improvements.

Legend:
- ☐ High-level
- ☐ Mid-level
- ▨ Foundational-level

I. RECIPROCAL MINDFULNESS:
They can help others to understand their potential and ability to self-regulate.

II. SELF-ACTUALIZED MINDFULNESS:
The child has acknowledged their potential, and frequently use methods to identify and adjust their emotions and arousal.

III. AESTHETIC MINDFULNESS:
While still addressing challenges, the child expresses compassion and an appreciation for others and the environment around them. They display an understanding of their ability to adapt and adjust their self-regulation.

IV. COGNITIVE MINDFULNESS:
The child has an understanding of their challenges with self-regulation. While they continue to have difficulty, they are curious and have a sense of exploration and make occasional attempts to adjust their emotions and arousal. Display an understanding of their ability to adapt and adjust their self-regulation.

V. SELF-ESTEEM:
The child makes frequent attempts at engaging with others and the environment. Yet, they appear to have poor social skills. They lack a sense of competence with required tasks and have difficulty following the rules. Hence, they have challenges in adjusting their emotions and arousals required for different activities.

VI. BELONGING AND SOCIAL ACCEPTANCE:
While the child may interact for short periods of time, they appear to lack empathy as revealed in challenges expressing emotions, affection, trust, and acceptance. Isolates oneself from the group or family system. The child has significant challenges inadjusting their emotions and arousal level.

VII. SAFETY AND SELF-PRESERVATION:
Child is focused on protecting oneself from physical and mental harm; desires routines and familiarity. Eloping or aggressive behavior is present. Proper engagement with the environment and others is limited. Poor emotional regulation, high arousal, and stereotypical behavior may be present.

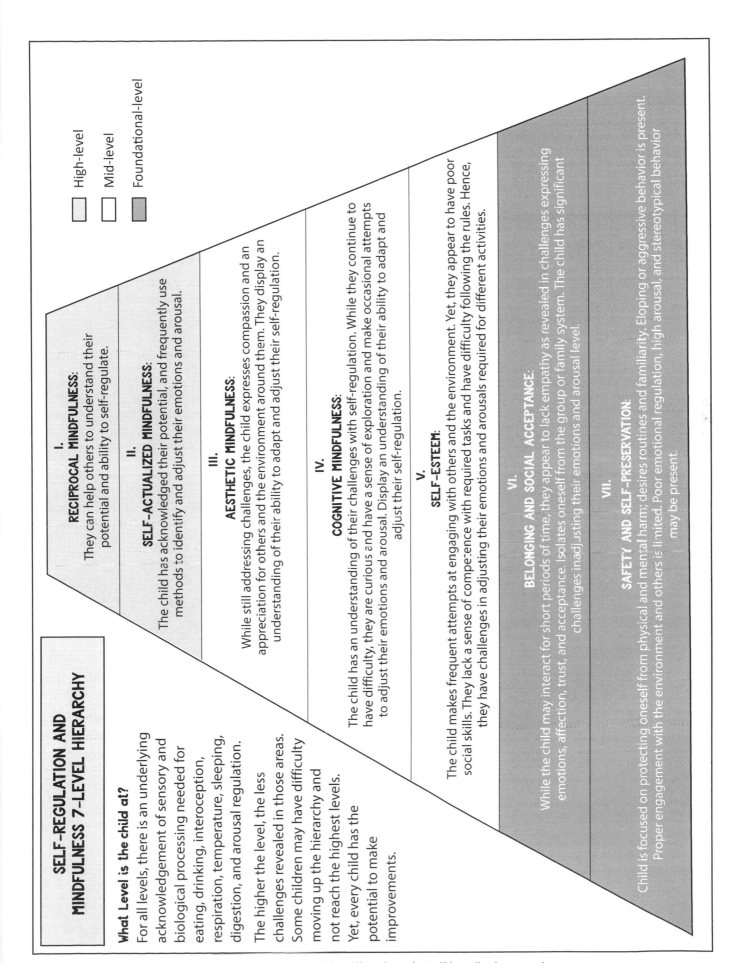

Part One

chapter 1

Let's Study the Brain

INTRODUCTION

Yes, all roads lead to the brain. However, it is important to also review the corresponding paths to get there. Let's think about the anatomy of the human nervous system. Please note that this information is not meant to replace or supplement a thorough review of neuroanatomy. In this chapter, we show the various neurological systems and the brain in a basic manner. We will start with the anatomy of trees. Yes, trees. While this may seem *disconnected* from the premise of this book, it will all make sense.

ANATOMY OF A TREE: OUR NERVOUS SYSTEM

Have you ever marveled at the wonder and beauty of trees? Trees go through various stages within their lives, as well as between seasons. My grandfather loved to practice gardening. One of his huge successes was an apple tree. I was not aware that he had planted seeds for an apple tree until one time when I came for a visit. It was simply amazing how out of nowhere, there was a yard full of plentiful, delicious apples.

The area in which my grandfather planted the tree was not the best location, in my opinion. There were apparent obstacles that would seem to halt the growth of the roots. Yet, the tree flourished, allowing my children to taste the fruits of my grandfather's labor.

Now, why are we talking about trees? Perhaps you have already made some conclusions. Our bodies need food and water, as well as other external input. We are like trees in that we take in information from the environment through our limbs as well as our eyes, ears, and our skin. There are several internal processes that result in sensation in the form of information navigating through the "trunks" and various "branches" of our nerves before reaching our brains. In order for us to grow and develop, we must participate in this process. Passive interaction will not result in one's growth and will hamper development.

When working with our children, we must think of them as we do of the trees. We do not view trees as stagnant. We do not look at them as lacking potential. We know trees are transformative. Their growth is sometimes

Brain Nugget

Photosynthesis is the process that nourishes trees. In our nervous system, our brain's ability to change and make new connections is called neuroplasticity.

unpredictable like that of my grandfather's apple tree. While we only see the external parts of the trunk and branches, there is a strong connection made between the tree and its foundation through the many roots that have developed over time.

This concept can be correlated to our nervous system: Like a tree, our nervous system is not static. Like roots, new connections are made and strengthened based on our relationship with the surrounding environment. Change and growth is always possible. Our nerves are like roots that can grow and make new pathways. What connections are made depends on the environment to which one is exposed and the context in which one exists. My grandfather's tree only grew because it was exposed to what it needed. He cared for it despite its less then optimal quarters.

Our nervous system is powered through communication with the various happenings around us. Sensory information, or rather, stimuli from our environment, is the source of it all! Think of sensory stimulation as the detection of changes in the environment and inside of the body. If the context remained the same, stimulation would not occur. But things do change, causing arousal in our bodies. The light, temperature, sound, and demands on our bodies are constantly changing, causing us to frequently adapt. Similar to the trees adjusting between seasons, our adapting to sensory stimulation is part of our survival. For us to be successful, the various aspects of the nervous system must work together.

Let's think about our nervous system as bifold, use the tree as our model. The tree's underground anatomy— the roots and the root hairs—is the tree's first point of contact with the environment before nourishment is delivered to the other parts. For humans, our sensory receptors are the first point of contact, and nerves send messages through our bodies.

Like the tree's roots and root hairs, our receptors detect changes in the environment and determine if the nerve should receive the information or not. The detected change must be substantial enough for the sensory receptor to respond. A sensory receptor reaches a **threshold** as the result of a *strong enough* or *long enough* change in stimulation to evoke a response. This change occurs through touch, taste, sight, smell, sound, movement, or alterations in our internal organs; sensory receptor stimulation initiates the sensory process.

The **process of sensory information** is as follows:

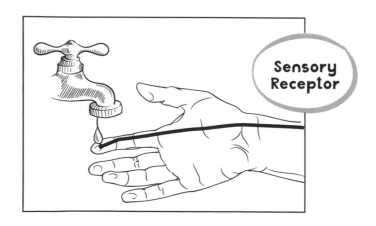

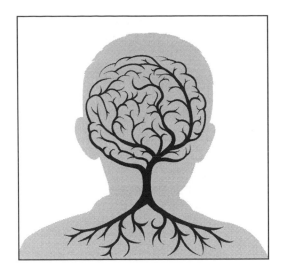

- The body detects a change, and the sensory receptors react.
- Information is then sent through nerve pathways.
- Messages regarding changes in touch or within our joints and muscles travel through the spinal cord.
- Hearing, taste, smell, and sight sensory stimuli enter through sensory receptors from various body parts, such as eyes, ears, and taste buds.
- Internal sensation from organs such as the stomach, lungs, and heart occur through receptors and nerves from those specific internal organs.
- Messages are then sent to the brain's various structures.

Like in the tree, the systems in the human body all must work together. Whereas anatomy courses teach us about the various subsystems in the body, the body as a whole, must work in synchrony. One subsystem cannot overpower another. When one does, dysfunction arises.

An image of a tree depicts a combination of the tree and the nervous system. The brain is infused with nerve branches and is connected with the body through its nerves. It communicates with the environment through the sensory receptors. A tree illustrates the subsystems as a working unit processing the information in the environment. If too little stimulation is presented, the sensory receptors will not react and will neglect to send the message. In such situations, information is not relayed to the brain.

Brain Nugget

Because the sensory receptors in our nervous system are located outside of the brain and spinal cord, this system is identified as the peripheral nervous system (PNS). The second component consists of the brain and the spinal cord. It is called the central nervous system (CNS).

A lack of sensory stimulation will negatively affect appropriate engagement. Under-water a tree, and the tree will not flourish. A person deprived of the necessary sensory stimulation, desired by their body, may lack appropriate interaction and engagement with others. Their maladaptive behavior may be an attempt to acquire what is deficient. The opposite occurs in the presence of too much stimulation—our sensory systems may become over-aroused.

A tree receiving too much water wilts and lacks vigor. A person receiving too much stimulation may also lack appropriate participation with others and their environment. Instead, their attention is focused on attempting to block out or avoid overstimulation. For humans, input to our bodies must be **"just right."**

Just as the various trees and plants in our environment each require different levels of input to flourish, we, too, vary in our needs. What each person needs is highly unique and dependent on the individual.

SO, WHAT HAPPENS FIRST? A TRIP THROUGH THE AIRPORT!

Sensation occurs first, then our bodies react to the sensory stimuli entering through the receptors. We have an extraordinary ability to attend to or block out stimuli. This helps us to prioritize what is important. The sensation has to catch our attention for us to feel and react. Have you ever found yourself saying "Did you hear that?" or "Did you see that?" only for the other person to respond "No?" For you, that stimulus was important, but the sound or sight that caught your attention was not powerful enough to catch the other person's attention. They were most likely focused on something else of importance to them. The system that controls this process is called the **Reticular Activating System (RAS).**

The RAS is like a gatekeeper. Its role is similar to the function of an airport security gate: It helps to filter out unwanted or unneeded sensory stimulation. The RAS acts as follows:

- **The RAS will allow in the information that is important to YOU!**
- All sensory information passes through the RAS, with the exception of smell.
- What information enters the RAS and how much depends on the person, place, or event.
- **Your arousal is affected by sensory input.** Depending on how much of the sensation and what stimulation enters, you will experience varying levels of alertness or rest.
- The RAS has output to the entire brain, spinal cord, and other important structures of our nervous system.
- The RAS is crucial for attention and decreasing distraction.

So, where is the RAS? It is located in the brainstem area.

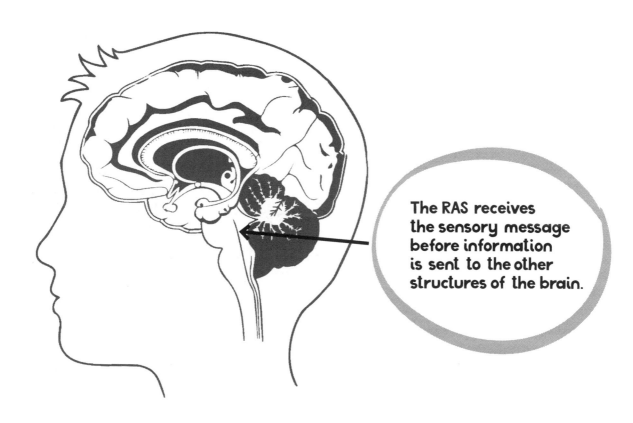

The RAS receives the sensory message before information is sent to the other structures of the brain.

Let us further explore the RAS. Think about going through airport security. Many people travel through the airport each day, some hours are busier than others. The morning brings a lot of people, while the late night sees just a few. Our consciousness operates similarly: We are wired to let in varying levels of stimulation depending on the time, event, or place. High facilitation when there is a lot of sensory information, moderate facilitation allowing for alertness and function.

Inhibition of stimulation allowing for rest and sleep RAS functions include the following:

- **Alertness and facilitation:** During the day, we allow more stimulation in, which allows us to perform daily functions.
- **Sleep and inhibition:** We need less stimulation when it is time for rest at night.
- **Attention:** You may also allow in more sensory stimulation during social activities, such as a nice outing with friends, versus sitting in a lecture or a work meeting.

The RAS also plays a role in the sleep/wake cycle, breathing, digestion, heart rate, muscle activation, and other functions vital to life. Your experiences and your focus on the environment program your RAS over time. Neurological deficits play a role in how a person's RAS functions: A poorly "programmed" RAS leads to poor interaction and behavioral responses.

So, let us go back to the airport security metaphor. As you know, only certain items are acceptable to bring on a plane, and others will not pass inspection. While one goal of security is to allow passengers to get through to their gates, another goal is to preserve safety and identify anything that could be a threat. The presence of a less than desirable item, such as a weapon, will cause an alert. In our RAS we receive an "alert" in the presence of a threat.

When there is a lot of information coming in at once, such as the sights and sounds at a children's party, our RAS becomes excited. In this case, excitement can be interpreted as either joy or fear. Either way, your body responds with heightened arousal. Similarly, if you hear a fire alarm, your RAS allows an increase in the amount of stimulation entering. This allows you to be hypervigilant in reaction to possible danger, it is a protective and vital process.

Dysfunction can occur at the RAS level. Some people's RAS lets in **too much sensory information** to process input efficiently. If the RAS does not limit the amount of stimulation entering, over-responsiveness can occur. Think about an invasion of people attempting to push through the airport security gates all at once. That could be an overwhelming situation. The person experiencing an influx of sensory stimulation may become over-aroused by all of the sensations approaching the RAS, and may have difficulty paying attention and prioritizing information. The person becomes hypervigilant and may be inattentive as they focus on decreasing or avoiding such overstimulation. They may also prefer activities that elicit more effective responses to help them to limit the stimulation and may seek out certain sensations and experiences.

Children with this sort of pattern are constantly in what we call **"fight-or-flight" mode**. It is the SNS that controls fight or flight reactions. When the RAS receives notice of a threat, the body automatically kicks into protection mode. The muscles tense, the pupils of the eyes dilate, and the ears become hypersensitive to sound. All of this happens from an automatic chemical release allowing the individual to see, hear, run, or fight for their survival. While this system is necessary, it is not needed at the same level of intensity that may have been required before modern times.

Unlike our cave-dwelling counterparts, there is not always a bear or tiger lurking behind the bushes ready to have us for dinner. But, our bodies still react to a nonthreatening stimulus, such as a sound, in the same manner as a life-threatening event because the RAS interprets the stimulus as something of importance or danger. It sends the alert out the SNS to allow the body to react and attend to the stimuli.

Brain Nugget

The "fight or flight" reaction is part of our nervous system called the autonomic system. The division is the sympathetic nervous system (SNS). The other division is called the parasympathetic nervous system (PNS). It is primarily responsible for regulation of vital functions such as heart rate and breathing.

Take a look into some children's eyes, specifically those with hyperactivity or hypervigilant behaviors. Their pupils are probably dilated, and their arms and legs are tense. They may overreact when you attempt to engage or touch them by crying or running away. Often, they have physiological responses such as sweating and breathing quickly. Some may even appear to enjoy stimulation, indicated by their engaging in frequent movement, climbing, and jumping.

These children seek these activities to utilize their stronger, more efficient sensory systems; seeking more stimulation activates the pleasure areas of the brain. However, when these children behave in ways to avoid personal interaction, it is an indication of their feeling unsafe. Such children are comfortable performing the gross motor activities that bring a sense of security, but anxiousness may be present, as they anticipate the possible presentation of undesired stimuli, such as your touch or voice. They may become angry or aggressive when you attempt to stop their seeking behavior.

The fight-or-flight system is constantly active in some children. Although the primary culprit is the SNS, the opposite division of the autonomic nervous system (ANS), the PNS, also plays an important role. The PNS is responsible for restoring vital functions of rest and digestion, among others. This division of the nervous system must communicate with the areas of the brain to assess the situation and then regulate breathing, heart rate, digestion, and muscle relaxation as appropriate.

When sensory dysfunction is present, the PNS may lack the needed activity that allows it to modulate the abundance of stimuli sent forth by the RAS. Because of this partnership between the RAS and PNS, all areas of vitality can be affected when dysfunction is present.

Dysfunction with the PNS includes issues with:

- Sleeping
- Eating
- Digestion
- Muscle tone

The child may:

- Be sensitive to light
- Dislike certain textures and touch
- Avoid or prefer specific foods
- Present as socially awkward
- Be aggressive at times
- Have gastrointestinal dysfunction, as in constipation or diarrhea
- Experience frequent illnesses, such as respiratory infections, due to stress on the body

Dysfunction occurs when sensory pain receptors become overly involved in processing stimulation. Due to the muscle tensing caused by the SNS, the pain receptors may react in the presence of a nonthreatening sensation, such as light touch. Increased pupil dilation may lead to painful responses to artificial light. In these situations, the RAS sends out an alert, resulting in an ongoing cycle, leading the person's RAS to be "wired" to be on the lookout for such threats. It may even react with simply the idea or anticipation of undesired stimuli making a strong connection to our emotions.

This becomes a challenge for many children. Perhaps they cry in the presence of certain food, entering a new environment, or being taken away from a desired activity. These emotional responses are the children's attempt to protect themselves from undesired stimulation, so stress and anxiety play a big role in the behavioral reactions we see with some.

There are motor behaviors related to the activation of the RAS— "*sensory in . . . motor out!*" Equilibrium, posture, and eye movements are functions directly influenced by the RAS. If the processing of the incoming information lacks efficiency, the output will also be inefficient. Children with dysfunctions in sensory processing (i.e., SPD, Autism Spectrum Disorder, ADHD) may present the following:

- Poor sitting posture
- Challenges with sitting tolerance
- Poor balance
- Difficulty with coordinating gross motor and fine motor activities
- Challenges with coordinating head, trunk, and eye movements for functional tasks (e.g., sitting at a desk and looking at a classroom board)

Primitive reflexes in some children, often present at the start of life (i.e., in babies and toddlers), that may integrate to functional movement as the child gets older. Retained primitive reflexes may present as the child has difficulty sitting against the back of a chair and appearing "wiggly"; a child not able to master the bilateral skills (i.e., being able to using both sides of the body together, also called "crossing the midline") or having trouble integrating movement in the upper body and the lower reflects further dysfunction. Hypervigilance and sensitivity to light, sounds, and tactile stimuli are additional indicators of retained primitive reflexes. For such children, activities such as gross motor games, handwriting, and self-help skills (e.g., shoe tying) are a challenge.

Distinguishing between the various characteristics of stimuli becomes complex due to the receipt of too much sensory information and a lack of filtering by the RAS. Distinguishing hot from cold and soft versus prickly or being able to identify an object through touch are compromised. Children with retained primitive reflexes may have difficulty finishing assignments on time, have sloppy desks or lockers, or have trouble sequencing activities from start to completion. Again, anxiety and stress come into play. The cycle of the overactive RAS continues. These are just a few examples of poor integration of primitive reflexes.

When a child feels safe, the PNS allows for social interaction and participation with the environment. If the RAS is overresponsive to a stimulus, the child presents with protective behaviors due to fight-or-flight activity. Many patterns of behavior we witness in children stem from self-preservation.

If something causes discomfort, the child will seek out what leads them to a sense of **security**. Even when a threatening stimulus is not present, discomfort could occur if the child does not receive enough of the desired stimuli, and the anticipation of the stimulus leads to anxiety and stress. When the RAS receives what it craves, the result is a **good feeling** or a **sense of well-being** produced by the internal chemicals released. The child will seek out the stimulation that works best for them to produce this good feeling. If they typically get a good reaction from spinning, they will seek out spinning. If crawling under the table and plugging their ears works best, that is what they will do.

Some children are on the extreme ends of the spectrum: It all depends on their protective measures. That is why some of the same interventions work for a variety of children. The differences lie within what happens internally. Our goal must be to change the child's focus. **The child will use their most efficient method of feeling good.** They are not interested in exploring new ideas that may cause stress.

Provide novel experiences and methods to help them navigate and participate. Let them know that liking movement is a good thing or that disliking certain textures or tastes is okay. The child must learn to allow for new and challenging opportunities. We start with addressing the **least-threatening sensory areas**.

When we help the child to make changes to behaviors related to certain sensory areas, the RAS has an opportunity to expand its focus from a few primary areas to other sensory systems. The RAS can then properly communicate with the PNS and not so much with the sympathetic division, dampening the heightened arousal state in the brain. Then, the senses will start to work together to more effectively interpret the environment, with less emphasis on what is in excess or missing.

Now, the first step in implementing this concept is teaching the child. They must gain an understanding of how their body works and the possibility of making changes.

First you have a feeling (i.e., sensation), and then you have an emotion. The emotion is the result of the feeling. There are areas in the brain that are specific to our emotions. The feelings, or sensory stimuli, coming into our body must go through the brain area regulating emotion before the message can continue to the higher areas of the brain. There is a guide, or relay station, that then directs the information to the various parts of the brain for it to make sense of things and produce a response. However, it is not that simple. Our emotions are a powerful thing! That part of our brain is very primitive and highly "wired."

THE APPLE: OUR EMOTIONAL BRAIN

Picture a stem connecting an apple to the tree. As the apple hangs off of the branch, anything traveling through the tree must reach that stem area first, then enter inside the apple. Let us think of the stem as the **RAS**. The apple is like the emotional part of our brain, deep inside of the largest part of the brain. Any information received from the outside world goes to the RAS and then to the emotional brain area. Which is why you have a feeling before an emotion and an emotion before you have a thought.

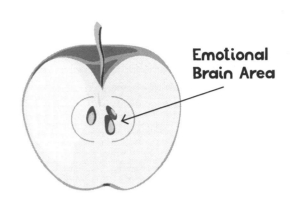

Emotional
Brain Area

Brain Nugget

The "emotional brain" is called our limbic system. It consists of the amygdala, which helps identify the emotion, encodes it, and communicates with the hippocampus, which stores the emotion. Another region of the limbic system is the septal region, which connects to the hippocampus to identify pleasure and a sense of reward.

When a message reaches our emotional brain, the various structures of that area go to work. They investigate whether the stimulus is something of pleasure or distress. Such information is categorized and then filed away in our storage cabinets so we know what to do when presented with similar stimuli. Memory and emotions are connected, the stronger the emotion is, the stronger the memory.

Emotional reactions can be automatic, similar to a reflex. For example, a classmate hits a peer on the arm. The child's RAS sends out a message that there was a physical threat. The emotional brain may then respond with fear or anger, and the response is to strike back. Unfortunately, the original "threat" may have simply been another child running and accidently bumping into their peer. This example is one in which there was not a lot of thought or planning: The reaction to hit was not appropriate and caused distress to the child and others around them. This is the **"short path"** of fear (i.e., an automatic response to a stimulus rather than a thought-out one), which is closely connected to the fight-or-flight reaction.

The structure which directs sensory information throughout the brain, is called the **thalamus**. Now, think about the process of information traveling from the sensory receptors to the RAS and finally to the emotional brain. It takes a lot to get a message delivered to the higher areas of the brain. Once we get through the feelings and the emotions, the information travels to the top.

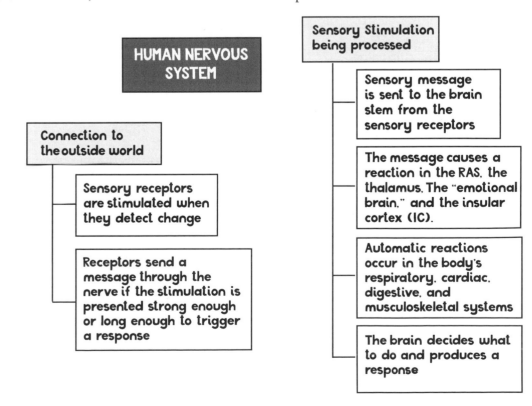

Brain Nugget

The "short path of fear" is the direct pathway to the amygdala. The "long path of fear" is the indirect pathway to the amygdala.

While the emotional brain is powerful and reaction time can be quick, there are methods to incorporate rational thoughts in combination with feelings and emotions. The frontal areas of our brain develop over time. Our ability to make decisions, choose between right and wrong, initiate actions, and stop ourselves from negative behaviors comes from the most prominent front part of our brain. Yet, these abilities are hampered in the presence of fear, stress, or anxiety.

Research shows a decrease in cognitive abilities in conditions that cause excesses of these emotions. However, the **"long path of fear,"** which involves the thalamus, sends the fear information to the front part of the brain to make sense of things. It takes longer but allows for a better outcome when a true threat is not present. The feeling, or sensation, occurs first, then an emotion. If all works well, then a thought should follow.

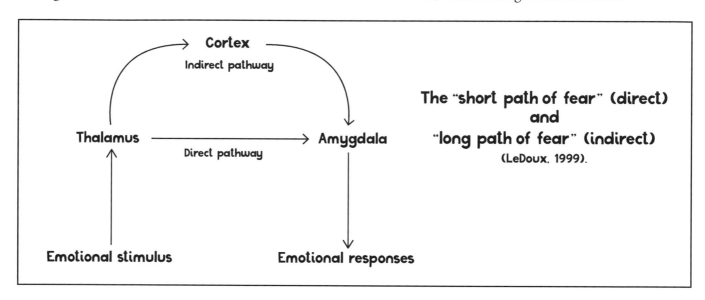

The "short path of fear" (direct) and "long path of fear" (indirect) (LeDoux, 1999).

If the RAS receives the sensation it desires, then a release of **good feeling** chemicals (known as endorphins) occurs. The natural chemical release is connected to a neurotransmitter called **serotonin**. In addition, when we go beyond the sense of well-being and interpret a feeling of accomplishment or euphoria as a direct result of performing an act, the **reward circuit** is triggered. When this happens, another neurotransmitter called **dopamine** is released in our bodies. We then have a sense of pleasure. This cycle becomes stronger the more we present ourselves with the stimuli that result in the release of dopamine, which then reinforces the behavior.

You may see how this cycle could lead some children to constantly seek out the action leading to pleasure. It may present in a somewhat addictive manner. Some children may have figured out that self-injury, such as biting their hand, banging their head, or slamming their body on a surface, can lead to an endorphin release. Also, self-stimulatory actions like flapping one's hands may produce a feeling of pleasure.

In addition to having an addictive quality, these behaviors can result in avoidance of undesired feelings and emotions. To break the cycle of pleasure seeking and avoiding behaviors, such as self-injury, the reward circuit must be changed. More long-term sensations of pleasure must replace the short-term effects these children get from inappropriate actions. The activities in this book are geared to produce a sense of well-being and internal reward.

THE "LEADER"

Think about how your brain is positioned in your head. The part of the brain that is just beneath your forehead is the **frontal lobe**. It is the "leader" of the brain. The most superior part of this section of the brain, just at the tip, is the **prefrontal cortex**. Being flexible in one's thinking, making decisions, using judgment, inhibiting unwanted or negative actions, problem-solving, planning, and making sense of emotions all happen in this area.

> ### Brain Nugget
> The cingulate gyrus connects the frontal lobe, the IC, and the limbic system. It is considered part of the limbic system.

The long path of fear involves the prefrontal cortex, which is important for the proper assessment of stimuli. Once the prefrontal cortex has reviewed the factors pertaining to the event, it can generate an appropriate response. There are structures inside the brain that connect this area to the emotional brain. They help you reappraise what occurred, specifically in the presence of negative stimuli and pain. While a lot of emphasis is given to the prefrontal cortex, some forms of therapy may not work for the child with neurological dysfunction. Some intervention strategies that emphasize conscious activation of the front part of the brain to help children learn to control their emotions remain ineffective for some.

One major structure is the **insular cortex (IC)**. The IC is an amazing structure of the brain, located close to the emotional brain area and just below the front part of the brain, it is our "self-regulation" hub. The sensory, emotional, and executive function paths all make a stop at the IC. The functions of the IC directly align with the goals of mindfulness in that the IC increases activity during self-awareness of one's emotions. Attention, making moral decisions, consciousness, self-awareness, interpersonal experience, empathy, and regulation of vital processes are just a few of the functions identified in the IC (Augustine, 1996; Hermans et al., 2011; Kurth et al., 2010; Menon & Uddin, 2010; Nieuwenhuys, 2012).

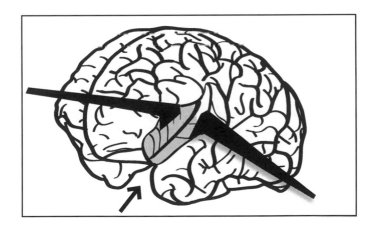

The IC mostly receives information from the emotional brain. It has a strong connection that allows us to produce socially appropriate responses to sensory input. Some consider the IC to be part of the emotional brain system. Various neurological conditions, such as autism, have been correlated with dysfunction in the IC (DiMartino et al., 2009; Menon & Uddin, 2010; Wylie & Tregellas, 2010).

While the prefrontal cortex produces more conscious responses, the IC produces unconscious ones. Following are some facts about how the IC functions:

- The IC produces physiological activation of pleasure and pain reactions in connection to emotional stimuli.
- Activity in the IC changes between experiences and environments.

- The IC sends pleasurable sensations as a result of the person doing the "right thing" or making others happy. This is the connection to empathy and concern about others' well-being.
- The IC is involved with **inhibition sensations,** which occur in the presence of socially inappropriate behavior or causing others distress. In such cases, the pain sensations are necessary to inhibit the undesirable activity.
- Dysfunction of the IC may lead to poor modulation of sensory input, hyperactivity, and painful over-responsiveness.
- Dysfunction in the IC also may possibly align with stereotypical behaviors seen in conditions such as Autism. The IC may lack the activation needed to appraise incoming sensory information, pain responses may occur during typical social activities or interaction. Children with such impairments may attempt to use more developed and efficient motor areas to block out the unwanted pain responses.

The undesirable visceral reactions sent from the IC can lead to pain. This connection between the IC and pain is due to the IC's relationship to one of the strongest and largest nerves in our body, the **vagus nerve,** or cranial nerve X. It is called the **"wandering nerve,"** as it has connections with most of our organs and is the only nerve that starts in the brain and exits to the rest of the body. It detects sensory changes related to rest and digestion and produces motor responses. For example, it may detect changes in the nervous system and become activated to regulate breathing and heart rate. **The vagus nerve terminates in the IC.**

A functional IC measures the degree of pain to calibrate appropriate responses. When dysfunction is present, persistent and prolonged pain responses can be triggered. So, individuals may experience gastrointestinal complications, such as irritable bowel syndrome, or the gastrointestinal problems seen in children with developmental disorders (Chaidez et al., 2014; Hsiao et al., 2013; Mazurek et al., 2013; McElhanon et al., 2014). A significant number of children with Autism also have issues with digestion, constipation, and food sensitivity. An appropriate function of the IC is to acknowledge a full bladder. Dysfunction can lead to the challenges many children face with urinary control. Furthermore, the IC plays a role in smell and taste sensory input. The limited dietary choices of some children could be the result of a lack of the activation in the IC needed to appraise the stimuli and hamper pain responses.

In terms of executive functioning, the IC is involved with risk assessment. It is constantly waiting for unpredictable or unwanted stimuli (Seymour et al., 2007) and is an important component in avoiding risk-taking. The major role of the IC is to connect internal self-awareness with the external world. How others view us, repercussions for our actions, and desiring to do the right thing encompass its major functions. Some of the hyperactive, sometimes dangerous, behaviors in children with ADHD, SPD, and ASD are directly related to the IC, as is the lack of empathetic behaviors some may display.

Activation of the IC can lead to improved interactions with others and self-actualization. Mindful practices and sensory stimulation can improve IC function. Individuals who practice meditation reveal enlarged ICs. They show increased body awareness and acknowledgement of their emotions. Deep diaphragmatic breathing, controls movement of the body, and use of temperature-based input could enhance the activity of the IC and self-regulation overall.

But remember, we have two sides of our brain. There is a left side and a right side, each including a replica of the IC and the other structures. There are slight differences on each side of the brain. The left side is involved more in reasoning and logistical thinking, whereas the right side is more intuitive and involves emotions and creativity. This is also important in the IC. The left IC is found to be involved in verbal memory activities. The right IC is highly important to sensory perception, emotion, and aspects of executive functioning.

Don't allow this to make you believe one side of the brain is "better," or more necessary than the other. You need both to work together. For example, the left side of the brain is involved in understanding language.

But, you would miss out on the emotional aspects of language if the right side of your brain were damaged. Hence, integration of both sides is key.

I am sure you can identify a child whom you perceive to be more "right brain" than left, and vice versa. This is evident in their physical functioning. What occurs in the brain is revealed through the body. This is an aspect of the mind-body connection. The **brain** is the structure, and the **mind** is the result of the activity in the brain. The mind-body connection allows the body to influence the brain and the brain to influence the body.

Brain Nugget

The functions of the right versus left hemispheres of the brain refer to Brain Lateralization.

chapter 2

The Science Behind Self-Regulation & Mindfulness

This section begins to outline some of the history behind specific conditions and diagnoses. Although you may have chosen to read this book because of a child of concern, the information pertains to any and every child as we explore self-regulation and the benefits of mindfulness approaches. I encourage you to keep your mind open, the evidence may directly relate to a child in your life. Surprisingly, that child may or may not be the one you initially intended to help. You may discover that the findings can relate to most children. This allows the techniques to be easily applied in different scenarios, as we can share the principles with an entire classroom or simply one child. However, to start, we will directly review the history of SPD, ASD, and ADHD. Some of you work in the fields of occupational therapy, speech language pathology, or physical therapy. The next section, on the history of multisensory integration, is likely already familiar to practitioners.

SENSORY PROCESSING DISORDER

Sensory integration is the organization of sensation for use.

—Dr. Jean Ayres, *Sensory Integration and the Child, 1979*

Let me start by reiterating that self-regulation comprises a few factors, one being **multisensory integration**. Jean Ayres (1963) is a name known by many occupational therapists. She was a true pioneer, being the first to use the term **sensory integration dysfunction**. Dr. Ayres acknowledged the connection between the nervous system and the behaviors seen in individuals of all ages. **If the information from the environment enters the individual's sensory system in a disorganized fashion, the produced behavior would in turn be disorganized**.

Ayres theorized that therapy interventions needed to first target the "emotional brain." She knew one had to meet the child at their level and find their motivation. As she worked with children having challenges in learning and social behaviors, Ayres claimed that by targeting the innate and automatic sensory system, one could address the deep-rooted neurological causes. Successful integration of the senses, motor input, emotions, and cognition is necessary for successful engagement and participation. Changes in the brain occur as a result of presenting the "just-right" challenge in various forms of fun and playful sensory stimulation.

Children presenting with sensory challenges may be identified as having **SPD**. They may or may not have an additional diagnosis, such as ASD or ADHD. Miller and colleagues (2007) offered an updated nosology identifying three major classifications of SPD. To start, *sensory processing* is the suggested term when referring to the child's disorder. Miller and colleagues described the major patterns seen in children with SPD: They present with dysfunction in sensory modulation, discrimination, and sensorimotor activity. In summary, children with SPD may display the following:

> ## Brain Nugget
>
> SPD is not recognized in the American Psychiatric Association's Diagnostic and Statistical Manual of Mental Disorders, 5th edition (DSM-5®; 2013). Those acknowledging the disorder identify three patterns of SPD: Sensory Modulation Disorder (SMD), Sensory Discrimination Disorder (SDD), and Sensory-Based Motor Disorder (SBMD).

- Challenges responding to incoming sensory stimuli and adaptation to the demands of the sensory stimulation presented

- Inappropriate emotional responses, social behaviors, and ability to functionally attend to a task

- Challenges in sensory modulation, may lead to the appearance of defensiveness or under-arousal or to the seeking of sensory stimulation

- Overreactions to sensory input secondary to taking in sensory information too quickly, or for an extended timeframe

- Symptoms may be identified as hyperactive or inattentive

- Difficulty with sensory discrimination; interpreting the 'where' and 'what' in regards to sensory stimuli

Perhaps one of the most overlooked aspects of SPD surrounds those with motor activity concerns. Due to lack of coordination of the various sensory systems, children with SPD may appear clumsy or disorganized. Children with such disorders also may be mistakenly assumed to have ADHD due to decreased strength in or control of their trunk, which can make it difficult for them to "sit still" for periods of time (Miller et al., 2007).

With all of the SPD patterns mentioned, dysfunction in the brainstem affects the child's ability to activate higher-order brain functioning. The RAS and IC play a vital role. The lack of filtering of sensory stimulation can lead to too much erroneous input through the RAS. The resulting behavioral patterns reflect the child's coping mechanisms in response to unwanted stimulation, which are strategies that align with stronger, more intact, systems.

A child with a strong motor system will seek movement to organize their sensory systems. They will block out the undesirable stimuli through gross motor activities. A child with an overactive vestibular system does not have that option. When presented with movement, the IC may produce a painful visceral reaction. The child's response may be to cry or elope from the presented stimuli. Some children receive so much information through the RAS they are unsure to what component they should attend and may be distracted and inattentive. Lastly, with an abundance of sensory information or a lack of filtering, children will have poor posture, visual processing, and motoric output. They appear clumsy and disorganized and may seek movement versus static sitting.

AUTISM SPECTRUM DISORDERS

There are many common symptoms between SPD and ASD, and many children with ASD also have SPD. The term *Autism* was coined in 1943 by psychiatrist Leo Kanner. It is derived from the Greek language and means "self" or "self-determination." Before Kanner's efforts to define Autism, it was noted that some children presented with very egocentric, personalized lives. The symptoms, including poor social skills, communication, and engagement with others, puzzled professionals and families during that time.

Over the years, the definition of Autism evolved. Initial descriptors highlighted the varying challenges in speech, social, and behavioral skills (Kanner, 1943). When Kanner (1943) first coined the term *Autism*, he intended to appease the curiosity around a group of puzzling symptoms in children. Such children displayed peculiar behaviors and abilities. They had an affinity for music and unusual memory recall, yet were self-absorbed. The perplexing condition also included behaviors such as a desire to spin objects, a lack of response to affection, and rigidity to change and other symptoms, such as repetitive verbal utterances and behaviors, echolalia, and over-responsiveness to sensory stimuli. Initially, many compared the syndrome to childhood schizophrenia. They also correlated the symptoms to high intellect in the parents and a lack of parental warm-heartedness. In years to follow, these ideas were debunked, and theorists embraced a consideration of neurobiological causes. A myriad of symptoms and severity levels led to an acknowledgement of the condition's complexity (Wing & Gould, 1979).

Currently, the symptoms of Autism are categorized as social communication and repetitive restrictive behaviors (American Psychiatric Association, 2013). They encompass the primary deficits of the diagnosis, but while Kanner was puzzled by Autism in the 1940s, we still remain somewhat unclear about the condition today. There are a multitude of treatment methods, theories, and approaches to addressing the symptoms of ASD. Parents may have feelings of confusion and become financially strained in an attempt to help their child navigate societal demands, and the cause of ASD remains unknown. We do know there is a genetic link with identified genetic mutations, hundreds to be exact. Mutations range from minor to severe; given the term *Spectrum* in ASD and the uniqueness of symptoms among children diagnosed (Chung, 2014). Each child is unique, which is why treatment and interventions are complicated.

ATTENTION DEFICIT HYPERACTIVITY DISORDER

Like ASD, our understanding of **Attention Deficit Hyperactivity Disorder (ADHD)** has evolved and continues to evolve.

Even now, we do not know enough to definitively say which treatment interventions work best for ADHD; however, we live in a wonderful time of advancements for addressing the disorder. Brain imaging, biofeedback, and clinical research are teaching us a lot. This book provides evidence-based and expert-driven anecdotal evidence for activities that support the needs of children attempting to live a purposeful and meaningful life with ADHD and the other-mentioned conditions. It is important to keep in mind that because the diagnoses of SPD, ADHD, and ASD, are all fairly new, they are continuously being investigated and finding new strategies that are proven and effective.

DEFINING SELF-REGULATION: MULTISENSORY INTEGRATION, EMOTIONAL REGULATION, AND ASPECTS OF EXECUTIVE FUNCTIONING AND MINDFULNESS

Self-regulation, sensory integration, emotional regulation, executive functioning, mindfulness … what do they all mean? When I think of my own self-regulation, I reflect on my ability to "get it together." We all become dysfunctional sometimes. My best example is when I had to sit for an exam for my doctoral candidacy. Well, I knew I had the information and knowledge required to ace the exam! Heck, I had studied the material for years! Yet, all of a sudden, the exam began and I felt my heart racing. I became sweaty and could not remember a thing. Not to mention, I knew that time was wasting away. I started to feel frustrated and disappointed in myself. Good thing I am an expert on self-regulation and knew exactly what to do! (I say that sarcastically.) In any case, I took a series of deep breaths, exhaling slowly, acknowledged my feelings and emotions, and started working—good self-regulation and mindfulness at its finest!

Self-regulation consists of multisensory integration, emotional regulation, and executive functioning. It comprises one's awareness and ability to control and adapt those functions: This is how I view the term and how I use it throughout this book.

My definition of *self-regulation* evolved based on the research of Albert Bandura (1991). His studies led him to define the triangle of *Reciprocal Determinism.* The model revealed the important interface of a **person,** the **environment,** and the person's **behaviors.** Bandura identified the influence of **cognition, physical factors,** and **emotions** to further explain a person's motivation and goal attainment. **Bandura's model is a major foundation for the science of self-regulation and for this program.**

Most of the suggested activities do not focus solely on how a child self-regulates: Many of them demonstrate to the child *how* to self-regulate through the observation of others' behavior. Bandura further provides insight into this concept by noting that people are influenced by others' behaviors and learn how to control their behavior through such engagement (Bandura, 1991). I identify this process as **reciprocal regulation.**

This notion is similar to those involved with training an infant to sleep and calm itself. Of course, the ultimate goal is for the child to have appropriate responses and strategies needed to participate successfully in their daily life. Yet, the caregiver also builds improved self-regulation through the process of helping the infant. The social rules and desires come into play. We have personal wants and needs that motivate our actions with the child. When the infant calms, so do we. If the child is upset, and hyper-aroused, we become anxious and agitated. Our arousal also affects how the infant presents. If we appear unhappy and lack patience, the child, too, may feel discomfort. They may feel uncertain of what to expect.

This concept of **reciprocal regulation** is highly important to how we approach our children. It is further grounded in the science of **mirror neurons.** Such neurons, allow us to acknowledge and sense the feelings of another person. A worthwhile goal is for our children to gain awareness of their arousal and emotions **and** to have empathy for others. As adults, being mindful of our own regulation is key to helping children learn to self-regulate.

Some children need more guidance and support to improve their self-regulation. For them, treatment requires the use of enhanced reciprocal regulation strategies. Multisensory integration, emotional regulation, and executive functioning remain the foundation and must **all** work together. *Mindfulness is a conduit for self-regulation.* Our earlier mention of the brain revealed that mindfulness techniques could enhance the areas vital to self-regulation, which include the IC and the prefrontal cortex.

Now that we have clarified our definition of *self-regulation,* it is important for us to first further explore the science behind the various components. We define **multisensory integration** as taking in stimuli through two or more sensory systems simultaneously and producing a functional and adaptive response. The key is that the process must be functional and adaptive.

What's more, the various senses must work in synchrony. We have vision, smell, sight, touch, and taste. The therapeutic terms we utilize for those senses are the *visual, olfactory, tactile,* and *gustatory systems.* Functionally integrating input from five senses in order to function seems complex enough; however, it does not stop there. There are also the vestibular and proprioceptive systems, interoception, and praxis.

The **vestibular system** is in charge of movement through space and interpreting changes in our head positioning. **Proprioception** is knowing where your body is in space and involves the joints and muscles. Another system is that of **interoception.** Some define the vestibular and proprioceptive systems as being components of interoception.

In this book, we define interoception as the internal sensations felt with the vital functions of hunger, thirst, and digestion. The processing of such input is primarily due to IC activation. Lastly, **praxis** involves having an idea and a plan and being able to execute it. This can involve movement and the visual system and systems controlling how one sequences activities. Taking all of these various systems into account, interpreting information around us requires a multitude of factors.

While there are different parts of the brain primarily responsible for interpretation of the various sensory systems, integration involves all parts of the brain and nervous system working together in synchrony. Once such synchronization occurs, similar to that of an orchestra, we are able to function in a unified, purposeful, and intentional way. When our sensory systems are not in synchrony, disorganization occurs. There are often challenges in being able to attend to stimuli: our arousal level becomes compromised in the presence of asynchronization. During such an event, we can present with hyperactive behavior—confused and frustrated— or simply become passive and shut down. Multisensory integration is the foundation of our existence.

Recent research further addresses multisensory integration, emphasizing that responses involving multiple senses working together result in greater responses versus sensory integration of one system alone (Alvarado et al., 2007). Stimulation of more than one sensory system at a time can enhance intervention and improve engagement with the surrounding world. Stein and Meredith (1993) developed **three principles based on their neurological research** that translate directly into these activities. Addressing our *Nine Targets* encourage stimuli of all of the sensory systems, with the goal of enhancing areas of weakness by coupling sensory areas to improve integration. As postulated by Stein and Meredith:

1. When different sensory stimuli are presented from the same location, multisensory integration is stronger.
2. When the sensory stimuli are presented at the same time, multisensory integration is stronger.
3. When the separate sensory stimuli are fairly weak in isolation, multisensory integration is stronger.

Let's look at the science behind **emotional regulation**. The term itself appears to be self-explanatory. If you were given the task of defining it, things become more complex: It is a very complicated phenomenon. There often is a negative connotation to the idea of *emotions* when we think of their regulation. Yet, emotions can be both "positive" and "negative."

Before you have a thought, you have an emotion. Emotions represent our ability to interpret information from the environment: Before we are able to process, interpret, and incorporate an idea, we have a feeling, and **how we react to that feeling/sensation leads to our emotional response.** How successful a person is at emotional regulation involves their ability to control the emotion that results from an experience or event. In some cases, this is not an easy feat. When emotions occur, there are reactions in the body, some of which may feel out of control and take over a person's functional ability.

Various emotions, such as happiness, excitement, and fear, can evoke the common physical changes of increased heart rate and respiration; however, the way we respond to these changes may vary. As Bandura (1991) revealed, our social learning dictates how we present and respond to feelings and emotions, resulting in behavior. We may define **behavior** as the physical response to a change in our feelings that is observable by others. A person must determine if it is appropriate to react to a particular feeling or attempt to suppress the physiological responses. As mentioned in Chapter 1, the IC plays an important role in our unconscious responses, and the prefrontal cortex is vital in the conscious response. Consequently, there is an obvious connection to **executive functioning**. The IC produces unconscious responses that allow for access to the inhibition of unwanted or inappropriate reactions.

We can apply techniques to activate the RAS and the IC to result in a desired physiological response. A primary example would be taking a deep breath when one's arousal has increased. Remember my test anxiety? Taking a deep breath may result in a decrease in arousal and unwanted visceral reactions.

The vagus nerve, the tenth nerve of the brain, is connected to our lungs to control respiration, to the heart to control heart rate, and to the stomach to control distention. The vagus communicates with the IC, which then connects with the emotional brain, and lastly, the prefrontal cortex responds by hampering the emotional brain's reactions. The process of having a feeling and allowing time to interpret it becomes an integral part of regulating emotions.

Jaak Pankseep (2005) stated that "... emotional feelings may reflect the neurodynamics of brain systems that generate instinctual emotional behaviors ... [this process] saves us from various conceptual conundrums." Our emotions are behavioral responses that reflect what is occurring in our brain and nervous system. Through his research with animals and humans, Pankseep identified seven core emotions. The **emotional systems** and related **internal feelings** are:

1. **SEEKING** (reward; enthusiasm)
2. **RAGE** (frustration)
3. **FEAR** (anxiousness/nervousness)
4. **LUST** (desire)
5. **CARE** (tenderness and love)
6. **PANIC/LOSS** (loneliness and sadness)
7. **PLAY** (joy)

This book utilizes Pankseep's feelings to help children and adults verbalize the corresponding emotions. For example, a person who is seeking something has the feeling of reward or enthusiasm. Rage can cause feelings of complete frustration and upset. Fear causes anxiousness or nervousness. Lust relates to a wanting or desire for someone or something. Care correlates with experiencing tenderness and loving feelings. Panic or loss relates to intense loneliness and sadness. And lastly, play results in joy.

This book clusters these feelings into two acronyms. The first is **FADS**: frustration, anxiety, desire, and sadness. The second acronym, **JEL,** includes joy, enthusiasm, and love. Our program's lessons address the underlying assumptions that FADS relate to short-term emotions. They are protective but can hamper successful engagement and interaction with others. Conversely, JEL emotions are more long term and lead to a sense of well-being.

Our emotions relate to a release of chemicals from the brain throughout the body. For example, with FADS emotions, neurotransmitters are released to relieve pain to provide an immediate sense of security. As a result of frequent chemical activity from these processes, one can become "addicted" to the reaction. For example, children who cry when being taken to daycare or a therapy session may have connected their emotions to a release of "good feeling" chemicals and may always cry when faced with similar situations: As mentioned previously with regard to FADS emotions, the release and good feeling are short term, so the child would have to repeat the event to evoke a similar reaction. With JEL feelings, the sense of well-being may be more continuous and long term: There is more of a sense of permanent security.

Given these examples, you probably already see a connection between sensory reactions and emotions. We receive sensory information from our environment, and there is an automatic emotional response or change in feeling. Most of this activity occurs in the lower-order brainstem regions of our nervous system. One of the most important aspects of this process is the earlier-mentioned term *executive functioning*. Executive functioning is key to the behavior one displays. We can make a conscious decision to respond to the emotions or simply let them take charge. Being able to have some control over our response occurs through activation of the higher-order areas of the brain.

Executive functioning encompasses problem-solving, attention, flexibility, inhibitory control, and reasoning. **Problem-solving** is one's ability to make decisions and come up with alternatives to address the situation. In order to problem-solve, you must first attend to the events that have occurred. The term *flexibility* refers to one's ability to change between thoughts and ideas and incorporate more than one concept at a time.

Another crucial piece of executive functioning is **inhibitory control**. When an emotional feeling occurs, initial reactions may not be the most appropriate. Executive functioning inhibitory control entails having the **judgment** to cease those reactions. Lastly, **reasoning** involves the interpretation of feelings and allows one to then devise a plan. As you can see, this is a multifaceted process. To utilize our executive functioning, we must first be able to acknowledge what is happening. We can then accept it, make a decision, and move forward. That brings us to mindfulness.

Mindfulness means "Paying attention in a particular way: on purpose, in the present moment, and nonjudgmentally" (Kabat-Zinn, 1994, p. 4). Being fully aware in the present moment includes **all sensation** and **emotions** in that moment— "Being a witness to one's own personal experience" (Napoli, Krech, & Holley, 2009). Earlier, we identified mindfulness as **"a conduit for self-regulation."** It allows one an opportunity for proper assessment of an event. After a person can recognize their feelings and emotions, they must allow time before reacting. Strategies such as meditation and deep breathing enhance one's mindfulness.

Breath has a direct effect on the autonomic nervous system, which controls regulation. Rhythmic breathing leads to increased self-awareness (Napoli, Krech, & Holley, 2009). Because of this, it is important for us, as the teachers of our children, to become mindful of our own self-regulation. Mindfulness allows the adult to become more aware of the child's needs and what works for them. It also allows children to see things from another person's view. Rather than comparing themselves to others, they appreciate their differences, which enhances empathy and compassion. Research exploring mindfulness programs for children has demonstrated that such programs result in significantly improved attention, decreased anxiety, and better problem-solving skills.

Unfortunately, high levels of stress and anxiety have become chronic in today's society. Frequent fight-or-flight reactions may cause high levels of stress hormones and illness in the body. Learning is hampered by decreased activation of the higher-order parts of the brain and higher activation of the areas surrounding the RAS (Badre & Wagner, 2002). Children under stress can become disorganized and present with poor self-regulation. Fortunately, mindfulness can address these problems: Through attending to the moment, focusing, and repeating mindfulness techniques, positive change can happen!

So, if we were to go back to the start of our conversation in this chapter, sensory information is paramount. How we bring in sensory information from the environment to our bodies starts a domino effect with regard to our feelings and responses. Continued interaction with the environment occurs following a generated response. We have to make continued adjustments and adapt to have meaningful experiences. **Just one method, principle, or protocol will not address the various components of self-regulation.** When working with children, we must have strategies to address all of these factors and variations.

Maslow's theory is a psychological one that explains basic humanistic motivation. The theory views motivation as a factor in growth and development. Maslow identified various levels of human needs: He saw basic vital needs as the first level, and self-actualization, realizing one's own potential, as the highest level (Maslow, 1943). Needs on the first level of the hierarchy, which include food, water, warmth, and rest, take precedence and are the first form of motivation for humans.

Maslow revisited his original model, adding cognitive, aesthetic, and self-transcendence needs at the top of the pyramid (Maslow, 1970). The premise of the hierarchy highlights growth as well as deficiency in the absence of fulfillment of one's needs. The pyramid structure implies that one must fulfill the lower-level needs before moving on to the higher levels. The theory further expands the idea that people are not in a fixed state but are constantly developing. However, when deficiency occurs, anxiety and stress present. Such feelings may lead to an imbalance and to dysfunction and hampered growth.

This program aims to provide activities that address various levels of needs. Because the program targets diagnoses such as ASD, it is crucial to acknowledge that children have levels of functioning across a

spectrum. Based on Maslow's hierarchy, sensory processing, and mindfulness theories, I developed the Self-Regulation and Mindfulness 7-Level Hierarchy. The model provides a guide for exploring and understanding the needs of our children. It is focused on fulfillment of their needs or lack thereof.

The model illustrated in the intro identifies each level. The bottom of the pyramid represents the foundation of **Safety and Preservation.** Ascension to the top of the pyramid leads to **Reciprocal Mindfulness.** It should be noted that **sensory processing and basic biological needs are always viewed as a motivation or deficiency, regardless of the person's general level of functioning**. For example, someone functioning at the highest level could have periods of dysfunction if they are in need of sleep or are hungry. The model describes each of the seven levels. When selecting activities for a child, you should have an idea of their general level of functioning as it relates to this hierarchy. Revisiting the model may assist in goal development and acknowledgement of gains.

chapter 3

Brain Posters
& Activity Sheets

It is crucial to be aware of the functions of the nervous system when working with children. Self-regulation requires individualized attention and active participation. Children must understand why they feel and react in a specific way. They must also know how their brain and nervous system grows. We must be creative and provide attractive tools and activities to engage children and their caregivers. Within this chapter, hands-on activities and lessons will assist in teaching children about their nervous systems as well as assist the therapist to explain concepts to parents and caregivers.

The following chapter provides a platform for you to teach children the concepts in this book. Various activities are meant to address the multitude of developmental levels in children. It may be challenging to use these activities with younger or cognitively impaired children, but it is always worth a try! Many children can surprise you with their hidden abilities. Even if a child is nonverbal, we should not assume we know their level of comprehension.

MY BODY

ACTIVITY LEVEL
- Foundational level to midlevel

ACTIVITY AIM
- Teach child about their body, sensory system, and connection to the brain

YOU WILL NEED
- Paper
- Crayons, pencils, or paint
- Provided printout

DIRECTIONS
1. Review the song "Head, Shoulders, Knees, and Toes."
2. Talk about the role each of the parts plays for our bodies.
3. Have the child draw a self-portrait using the image provided.

PRE-ACTIVITY DISCUSSION POINTS
- Share how all of our parts are important and strong.
- Talk about how we do not use just one part at a time. (You can provide examples, such as needing your eyes to look when listening.)

POST-ACTIVITY DISCUSSION POINTS
- Have the child share and explain their picture. See what is missing and help them fill in those items.
- Be sure to introduce the trunk or "belly area": We often miss this in our lessons on the body.
- Talk about our inside parts, such as the heart (feel the heartbeat), the lungs (take slow breaths), and stomach (discuss a full and empty "tummy").

OPTIONAL
- Discuss how our inside parts can become loud (fast heartbeat and quick breathing) or very quiet (slow heartbeat and slow breathing); causing us to be energized or tired.
- Have the child perform loud activities, such as running in place, then quiet ones, such as closing their eyes and sitting still.
- Review that sometimes we need to be "in the middle" between loud and quiet, such as in school or going to public places.

TREE

ACTIVITY LEVEL
- Midlevel to high level

ACTIVITY AIM
- Teach children about their sensory system and connection to brain development

YOU WILL NEED
- Paper
- Crayons, pencils, or paint
- Provided printouts (optional)

DIRECTIONS
1. Read the following pre-activity discussion points to the child. You can be creative and add to or revise the questions. You should be aware of the age and developmental level of the child. Review the **Self-Regulation and Mindfulness 7-Level Hierarchy** to best implement the activities relevant to the child's level.
2. Have the child draw their tree (using the printout if desired).
3. Use the post-activity discussion to guide the closing conversation.

MIDLEVEL

Pre-Activity Discussion Points
- Have the child reflect on a tree's appearance. Ask them the following:
  - How tall is a tree when it is first planted?
  - How tall does it grow?
  - How wide do the roots spread beneath the ground?
  - How does the tree grow? Does it eat food or drink water?
- Discuss how the tree grows using both water and sunlight.
- Share how we are similar to trees, in that we need food and water and also outside sensory stimulation. Provide examples of touch, sound, light, smell, movement, and taste.
- Share how trees have roots and we have nerves. Our nerves connect our brain to the world around us. However, there must be a balance. Sometimes, our surroundings don't allow for what our body wants. Too much or too little of anything can be a problem. Provide an example of how too much wind could cause stress on a tree, and similarly for us, needing too much movement could lead us to feel stress when asked to sit still. Or if we do not like certain sounds around us, we feel pain and fear and may want to hide.

- Lastly, have them draw their tree. Be sure they draw the roots, trunk, and branches. If they were a tree, how would their tree look? For example, have them draw a short or tall tree, one with lots of leaves or bare branches, etc.

Post-Activity Discussion Points
- Why did the child choose to draw their tree in such a way? Start a discussion about what you see. Have them explain how they often feel the way they felt drawing the tree during certain situations (i.e., at school, on the playground, in new places.)

HIGHER-LEVEL
- Perform the pre-activity items and drawing described previously.
- Have the child draw the environment in which they would like to plant their tree; for example, would it be around other trees, in a quiet forest, or in a park with children climbing and jumping off?

POST-ACTIVITY DISCUSSION POINTS
- Have the child share why their tree and environment looks the way it does.
- Talk about why a tree cannot have too much water or sunlight or too little. Then discuss the negative impacts of too much or too little arousal when it is time to learn or listen. Reflect on being "in the middle" when it comes to arousal.

OUR SENSES

ACTIVITY LEVEL
- Foundational level and higher

ACTIVITY AIM
- Teach children about the nine senses

YOU WILL NEED
- Small containers, such as baby food jars or sandwich bags
- Something for the:
  - Nose (flowers, potpourri, or cotton balls with dipped in essential oils) placed in a container
  - Skin (jelly, lotion, powder) placed in a container
  - Eyes (water and glitter or sand) placed in a container
  - Ears (bubble wrap, beans, or beads) placed in a container
  - Tongue (candy, salt, lemon) placed in a container
  - Insides (internal organs) (a straw to blow bubbles in a glass of water or inflate a sandwich bag)
  - Joints and muscles (a small, heavy object, such as a weight or a bag filled with beans or sand)
  - Body moving (instructions to nod "yes" and "no" or play "Simon Says")
  - Praxis (ideas, planning, execution) (the printouts for the child to place in order; instructions to create and perform a short pantomime or dance)
- Provided printouts
- Crayons or pencils

DIRECTIONS
1. Follow the Pre-Activity Discussion Points. If the child has difficulty with listening and understanding the content, move on to simply presenting the items, allowing them to experience each one regardless of their ability to discuss.
2. Present the items in the list.
3. After each item is presented, use the specific post-activity discussion point.
4. Have the child fill in the sense chart, if appropriate.

PRE-ACTIVITY DISCUSSION POINTS

- Explain that we are amazing creatures. We can smell, see, hear, taste, touch, move, and feel, both outside and inside of our bodies (heartbeat and breathing).
- Explain that those abilities are what we call *senses*.
- Tell the child that our bodies are like music: Everything works together to create something beautiful.
- Present each item, and ask them to identify the sense being used.

POST-ACTIVITY DISCUSSION POINTS

- Smell: What sense was that for? What did you smell? Did you like the smell?
- Touch: What sense was that for? Did you like the feeling of what you touched?
- Sight: What sense was that for? What did you see?
- Sound: What sense was that for? Did you like what you heard?
- Taste: What sense was that for? Did you like how that tasted? Did you like how it made your mouth feel?
- The inside senses (internal senses): What sense is that for? How did it make your insides feel?
- Joints and muscles: What sense was that for? How did it make your arms and hands feel?
- Body moving: What sense was that for? How do you feel after moving?
- Praxis (ideas, planning, execution): Have child place pictures in order on page 34. Discuss how they did with either placing the pictures in order or following instructions for pantomime or dance.

SENSE CHART

SENSE	ITEM RELATING TO THIS SENSE
1. Smell	
2. Touch	
3. Sight	
4. Sound	
5. Taste	
6. Inside Sense (Interoception)	
7. Muscle Sense (Proprioception)	
8. Movement Sense (Vestibular)	
9. Orderly Sense (Praxis)	

OUR BRAIN

ACTIVITY LEVEL

- Midlevel or higher

ACTIVITY AIM

- Teach children about their brain's structures and functions

YOU WILL NEED

- Crayons, pencils, or paint
- Provided printouts

DIRECTIONS

1. Read the following pre-activity discussion points to the child. You can be creative and add to or revise the questions. You should be aware of the age and developmental level of the child. Review the **Self-Regulation and Mindfulness 7-Level Hierarchy** to best implement the activities relevant to the child's level.

2. Use the first image provided to discuss the various brain structures.

3. Share the role each brain structure plays, as indicated. Provide examples.

4. Have the child use the second printout to color or label the different areas of the brain.

5. Use the points for post-activity discussion to guide the closing conversation.

PRE-ACTIVITY DISCUSSION POINTS

- Use the first image, on page 36, to talk about the brain: The front area is our leader (the prefrontal cortex). It helps us make choices and allows us to make changes to how we act. The emotional brain area is deep inside of the brain. It tells us what we feel. The RAS is our guard. It is in charge of what senses can or cannot enter our brain. The IC is our teacher. It tells us what is good and not so good, but we have to listen to the IC for it to do its job.

POST-ACTIVITY DISCUSSION POINTS

- Use different colors to color the brain in the second image on page 36.
- Have the child talk about each part of the brain and its role.
- Discuss how all of the parts need to work together. However, note that the emotional brain is very strong. You need other parts to calm the emotional brain, or else it can take over.

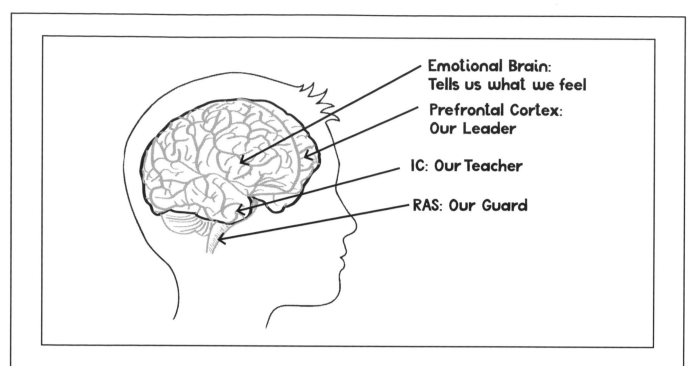

Emotional Brain:
Tells us what we feel

Prefrontal Cortex:
Our Leader

IC: Our Teacher

RAS: Our Guard

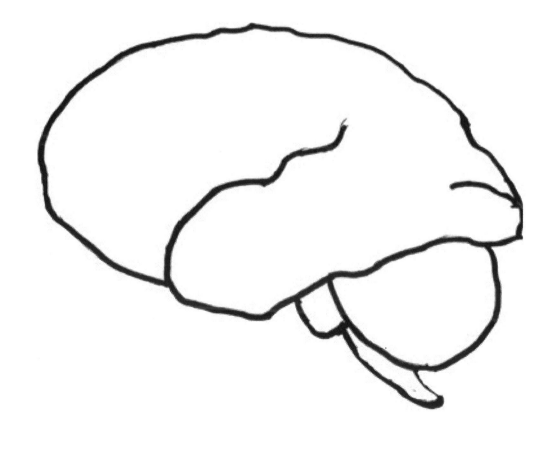

THINKING CAP

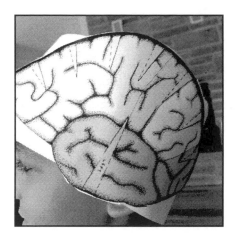

ACTIVITY LEVEL
- Midlevel or higher

ACTIVITY AIM
- Teach children about their brain

YOU WILL NEED
- Cardstock or paper plates, construction paper
- Glue, stapler, or tape
- Provided printouts

DIRECTIONS
1. Read the following pre-activity discussion points to the child. You can be creative and add to or revise the questions. You should be aware of the age and developmental level of the child. Review the **Self-Regulation and Mindfulness 7-Level Hierarchy** to best implement the activities relevant to the child's level.
2. Review the "Our Brain" activity on page 35.
3. Share the role each part of the brain plays as indicated. Provide examples.
4. Print the brain diagrams on cardstock or draw them on paper plates, and have the child cut them out if appropriate. Make a 2-inch-wide strip from construction paper, and staple the ends together to make a headband.
5. Help the child construct the brain "cap" by connecting the right and left sides of the brain to the headband (see photo).

PRE-ACTIVITY DISCUSSION POINTS
- Have the child identify the various parts of the brain and color the front parts. They can color the other structures as in the drawings on pages 38 & 39.
- Discuss how the lower and internal parts of the brain set the stage and are often in control: What happens around us and in our bodies reaches those areas first.
- Discuss that the front part of the brain (the prefrontal cortex) is the leader: It allows us to make a choice to listen to the body or do something else. It is up to us to let it lead! We can tell the other parts of our body to be quiet.

POST-ACTIVITY DISCUSSION POINTS
- Have the child put on their brain "cap" and remind them to put on their "thinking cap" every day.
- Review with them what happens when emotions take over.

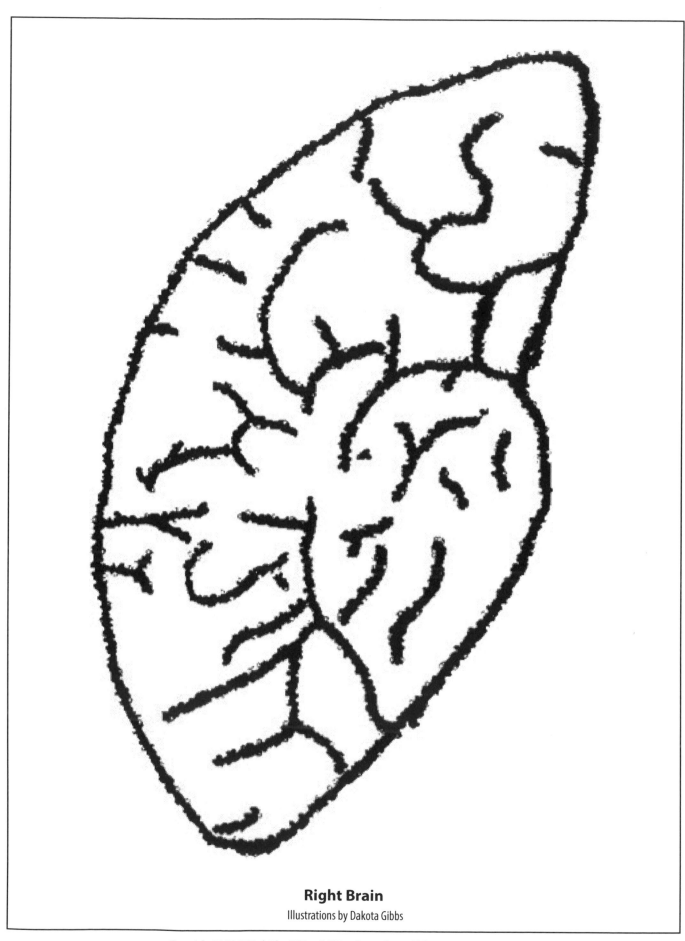

Right Brain

Illustrations by Dakota Gibbs

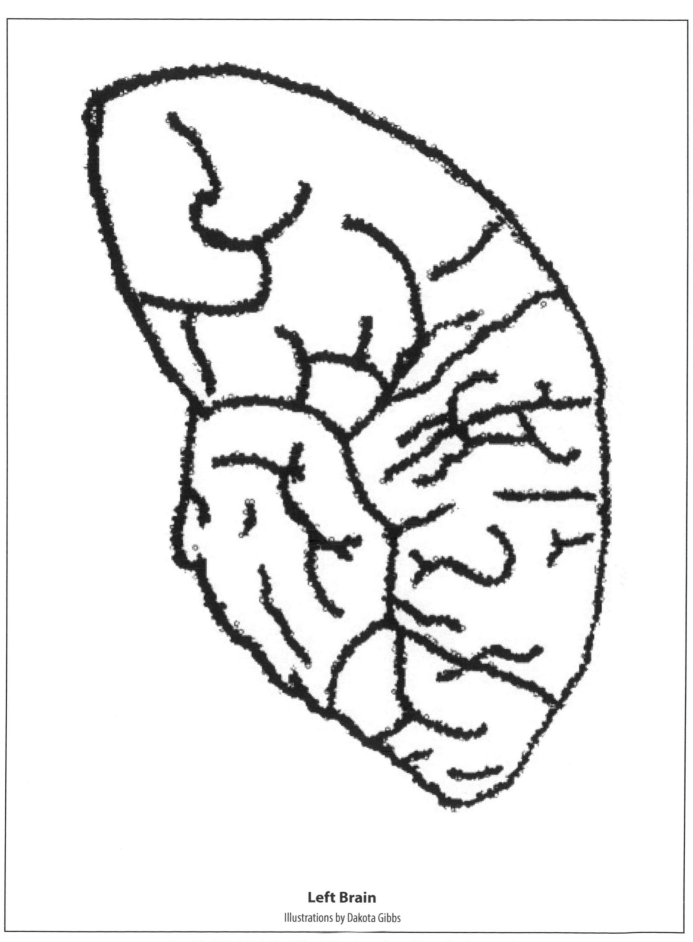

Left Brain

Illustrations by Dakota Gibbs

chapter 4

Arousal Assessments for Parents, Teachers, & Therapists

These assessments are not standardized tools, but they do provide a gateway to begin the exploration of the child's needs and desires. There are tools for therapists, parents, and teachers. The first section of the chapter provides an overview on arousal and threshold. Next, we explore possible underlying neurological components of the challenges our children face. This involves an in-depth look at primitive reflexes. Such information is geared toward professional licensed therapists or others working in collaboration with such professionals.

Last are hands-on activities for children and adults to use to perform self-assessments of self-regulation and learn new skills. Be sure to review the glossary in the back of the book to clarify specific terms. After gathering information from the assessments, use the daily targets to present the child with daily activities to help facilitate their self-regulation. Once you have knowledge regarding their arousal level, you can select activities that fit their needs while enhancing growth.

Before we get started on assessments, let's talk about our measurement tool. We will use a self-regulation and mindfulness "radio" called a **SAM box**. It allows us to identify our arousal level at a given point in time. Arousal relates to our breathing, how fast our heart is beating, activity level, and attention. To function and engage appropriately, we desire to be in the middle range. Once we experience high or low arousal, we need to do something to get balanced again. This is not a unique concept: The Alert Program® provides a great foundation for self-assessment of arousal levels.

Our SAM box simply provides an alternate tool for assessing arousal, emotions, and sensory integration. It uses terminology similar to that on the volume controls of a radio. I describe ways in which the SAM box is multifaceted, but you can use the SAM box to approach the child's arousal level. Following is an example of one way to use the SAM box for this purpose.

First, have the child describe their feelings in that moment. Ask the child to describe their breathing and heart rate. You can have them place their hand on their chest to provide additional feedback from their body. Provide examples of high arousal, such as heavy breathing and a fast heartbeat. Share how certain emotions can lead to heightened arousal. Then share that we call high arousal being "loud" on the SAM box. It is similar to a radio's volume being turned all the way up.

Next, do the same for low arousal. Talk about how low arousal may feel by having the child perform activities such as taking a deep breath and closing their eyes. Then share that the SAM box defines this as being "quiet." It is similar to having the radio's volume turned down. If the radio is set too low, you will not be able to hear it. If the radio is too loud, you will not be able to focus on anything else, as the sound is too distracting. For most of our activities, we need our volume to be somewhere in the middle.

Use the SAM box to look at the child's typical "volume" during play, school, or at home. You can then follow up by sharing how they can change their volume through what they do with their body! See chapter 6 to learn how to make your SAM box.

THRESHOLD AND AROUSAL OVERVIEW

It is important to note that some children have a form of SPD. They may also have another diagnosis, such as ASD or ADHD; however, the SPD diagnosis can stand alone. Children display various responses and behaviors depending on the environment, time of day, activity demands, and levels of rest and digestion. For all of us, there is a daily continuum of varying responses and arousal levels. Our diet, amount of rest, and activity levels result in our avoiding or engaging in certain behaviors, seeking or avoiding stimulation, and having periods of high arousal and low arousal.

Despite this continuum, there is often an overarching commonality. The following table provides an overview of some of the common themes children may embody. The **threshold** indicates how easily the child detects stimuli, or changes in their environment (low = quick detection; high = slow detection). A child's **arousal** is the behavioral reaction to stimuli that we can observe. Please note, there are other areas of sensory dysfunction not covered in this table, which primarily focuses on modulation.

Threshold and Arousal Levels and Treatment Intervention

	OVER RESPONSIVENESS TO SENSORY INPUT	UNDER RESPONSIVENESS TO SENSORY INPUT	CRAVING SENSORY INPUT
Threshold	Low; hypervigilant	High; inattentive	High; hyperactivity
Arousal	High; overreaction	Low; lacking a response	High; energetic
Preferences	Avoiding certain activities and preferring routine and predictable activities	Needing motivation and encouragement to attend to activities, especially gross motor play	High-intensity activities; risk-taking
Sample Treatment Activities	Slowly introducing new activities by pairing with nonthreatening preferred activities; weight-bearing activities; deep breathing; yoga; exercises moving from a flexed position to extension (to help reduce primitive reflexes)	Contrasting activities; fast versus slow; cold versus hot; high-energy activities, such as fast swinging, jumping, and crashing; strengthening activities if child displays decreased muscle activation due to lack of gross motor activities	Intense sensory activities, such as ice play; stimulating multiple sensory areas; swinging and crashing while listening to music; weight-bearing activities and intense input to the muscles and joints; deep breathing; yoga; meditation

From Miller & Schaaf, 2008.

PRIMITIVE REFLEXES

Primitive reflexes occur at the brainstem level. Such reflexes are observable during the beginning stages of life. They are involuntary reflexes to help a newborn through the birthing canal, assist with feeding, and allow one to learn how to move their body. Yet, they eventually integrate allowing for a coordinated sensorimotor system. Some individuals still present with observable primitive reflexes (Konicarova & Bob, 2013; Taylor, Houghton, Chapman, 2005).

Activation of the lower brainstem area may result in lack of activation of the front part of the brain and the other structures for movement, sensory processing, and learning. When primitive reflexes are evident, one may present with poor coordination, emotional regulation challenges, and difficulty attending to and performing tasks. For example, a baby reveals the primitive reflex called Asymmetrical Tonic Neck, or ATNR, when the head is turned. One side extends and the other one flexes. This can occur both in the upper and lower limbs of the body. If the reflex remains retained, children may have various challenges with school-based activities, balance and coordination, and visual activities. A school-aged child may display poor sitting positioning during tabletop activities.

The following chart identifies the various primitive reflexes, their function, and examples of dysfunction. After the chart, talk about how to test children for primitive reflexes. Most should not be evident after the first year of life. Activation and evidence of such reflexes should be addressed with appropriate therapeutic intervention. Professional consultation, with an occupational or physical therapist, may be indicated.

PRIMITIVE REFLEXES IN CHILDREN		
PRIMITIVE REFLEX	**FUNCTION**	**DYSFUNCTION**
Asymmetrical Tonic Neck (ATNR) Appears 18 weeks in utero, disappears around 6 months	Extension of one side of the body and flexion of the other to assist in the birthing process and later with reaching, eye-hand coordination, airway passage clearance	Poor balance; difficulty with coordinated eye movements needed for reading and writing; challenges in crossing midline of the body and separating the upper body and lower body movements
Symmetrical Tonic Neck (STNR) Appears 4–6 months, disappears around 8–12 months	Assists in preparation for crawling; when the child is on hands and knees, a flexed head results in legs extending; when the head is extended, the opposite occurs, with arms extending and legs flexing	Difficulty crawling on all fours; poor balance; clumsiness; difficulty with midline activities; poor sitting position—"W" sitting
Moro Appears in utero, disappears around 6 months	Occurs during the first breath of life; continues as a startle reflex in response to an unexpected stimulus or threat; the involuntary response is protective, as the infant is unable to distinguish threats; extension of the body (fall reaction), followed by full flexion (protective position), occurs spontaneously	Hypervigilant; overactive fight-or-flight reactions; sensitivity to light, sound, touch; poor emotional regulation; hyperactivity; poor attention to task; frequent illness due to a stressed immune system; fatigue
Spinal Galant Appears 20 weeks in utero, disappears around 9 months	Activates when either side of the spine of an infant is stroked; neck extension, hip rotation, and body flexion occur; assists with hip movement and rotation, specifically in utero and during the birthing process, as well as in the development of crawling.	Difficulty maintaining a seated position; constant fidgeting; bed-wetting and bladder accidents; sensitivity to touch and certain textures (clothing); challenges in following directions and with short-term memory
Palmar Appears 18 weeks in utero, disappears around 6 months	Assists in sucking, as the hands contract as the baby sucks; stimulation of the palms results in flexion or a grasp reflex; activation also leads to the mouth opening and jaw movement	Mouth movement as the child performs cutting, writing, or coloring activities; chewing on objects such as pencils; biting people; difficulty with grasp and speech due to tension in hands and mouth

PRIMITIVE REFLEXES IN CHILDREN

PRIMITIVE REFLEX	FUNCTION	DYSFUNCTION
Rooting Appears at birth, disappears around 4–6 months	Assists with feeding; baby will respond to stimulation of the cheek by turning toward the stroked side and opening mouth	Sensitivity in the mouth; challenges with food textures; messy eating; poor speech articulation
Tonic Labyrinthine Appears in utero, disappears around 4–6 months	Assists baby through the birthing canal; as head is flexed, the arms and legs extend	Difficulty coordinating body movement and eye movement; motion sickness; poor balance and posture; poor timing and sequencing (dyspraxia)
Landau Appears 3 months, disappears around 12 months	Head, legs, and spine extend when baby is held in the air horizontally; assists with muscle tone	Challenges with motor activities; high muscle tone (hypertonia) and difficulty learning; toe walking and lack of coordination; possible difficulty sitting against chair back; absence of the reflex during infant years indicates hypotonia and possible intellectual disability

Adapted from *Retained Neonatal Reflexes* (2005).

ASSESSMENT FOR LICENSED PROFESSIONALS OR THOSE IN COLLABORATION

ATNR	• Have the child get on all fours • Gently turn their head or have them turn it to the side and hold for 5 seconds repeat on the opposite side • Look to see if they can maintain the position or if they fall to the side opposite of the head being turned	
STNR	• Have the child get on all fours • Gently move or have the child move their head up and down and hold for 5 seconds in each position • Look to see if they can maintain the position, if they have excessive movement in their trunk, or if they are sitting back on their legs	

ASSESSMENT FOR LICENSED PROFESSIONALS OR THOSE IN COLLABORATION	
Moro	• Have the child stand with both feet on the ground and tilt their head back to look at the ceiling • You can also ask the child stand on one foot with their arms out to the side • Look for loss of balance and excessive movement
Spinal Galant	• Have the child get on all fours • Gently stroke the left and right sides of their spine • Look to see if they can maintain the position, if they have excessive movement in their trunk, or sitting back on their legs
Palmar	• Have the child stand with straight arms and ask them to wiggle their fingers • You can also have the child face their palms toward the ceiling; stroke the hand from the thumb toward the palm • Look for excessive wrist movement and movement in the mouth and/or tongue
Rooting	• Gently stroke the cheeks and the above the upper lip of the child approximately 3-5 times • Look for head movement towards the direction of the stroke and mouth opening and movement

ASSESSMENT FOR LICENSED PROFESSIONALS OR THOSE IN COLLABORATION		
Tonic Labyrinthine	• Ask the child to get on their belly, extending their neck, lifting chest slightly off of the floor, with arms extended behind and legs straighten and elevated • Look to see if the feet turn upward with flexed knees	
Landau	• Ask the child to get on their belly, extending their neck, lifting chest slightly off of the floor, with arms extended toward the front of the body and legs straighten and maintained on the floor • Remind the child to lift up their chest but keep their feet on the floor • Look to see if the legs leave the floor as in the image above	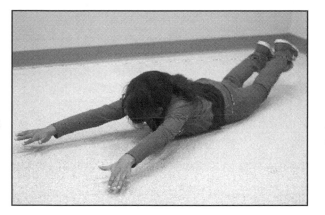

BIOMARKERS

Biomarkers are physiological changes in the body related to heart rate, responses from our nervous system, and breathing. Biomarkers can be monitored to help identify a child's typical arousal level and threshold response to stimuli.

Biomarker Assessments

The following biomarker assessments can be used for most children. It is recommended that you use these techniques in conjunction with a healthcare professional, such as an occupational, physical, or speech therapist. Basic application of these assessments may provide you with more insight regarding the child's arousal and threshold. The following are important considerations before beginning an assessment of biomarkers:

- Acknowledge the child's tolerance for touch, sitting, and participating in tabletop activities.
- The child needs to be able to sit still or lie down for at least 15 to 30 seconds. The child must also tolerate minimal touch for short intervals of time.
- Identify effective methods of communication: speech, pictures, gestures. The child needs to be able to follow directions, such as "look at me" or "let's sit for a minute."
- Obtain a penlight, stopwatch, and possibly a device to monitor heart rate (such as a sports watch that measures heart rate/pulse, which can be purchased inexpensively). The penlight will assist you in viewing the child's eyes. The stopwatch or heart rate monitor allows you to monitor the child's physiological response before and after selected activities.

<u>**Part I: Eye Test**</u> Changes in the eye's pupil occur secondary to light stimulation. Research shows that pupillary dilation (widening of the pupil) occurs during periods of excitation, such as in fight or flight (Moshe et al., 2014). Some children with high arousal levels have dilated pupils on a regular basis. Changes in size, such as when a light is shined at the child's eyes, would be minimal. In addition, irregular eye motor responses may be limited. Minimal eye reactions provide valuable information about the child's nervous system responses; for example, a minimal reaction to light may indicate that the child's fight-or-flight reactions are in constant overdrive or that there is a lack of flexibility or synchrony between the systems controlling regulation. Note that if typical responses are not seen, there may be a need to seek further medical evaluation. The eye assessment may also provide information regarding a child's progress in treatment: When improved eye reactions, such as an increased pupillary response to light and a smaller resting pupil size, are seen, this may indicate that interventional activities are working.

There is not a specific measure to look for when conducting the following assessments: Each individual child is unique. What you see in their reactions will inform you, and the child, about their arousal and threshold.

Position and Environment Have the child sit in a chair. The room should be dim. Face the child and have them look straight ahead. If needed, place an item of interest on the wall or have a video playing in the distance behind you.

What to look for:

1. Size: Pupil size should be similar in both eyes. Normal size is about 3 to 5 mm.
2. Accommodation: Look for the eyes to move inward toward the nose.
3. Look to see if there are any changes in the pupil. There should be an obvious change in pupil size from regular to dilated to contracted when presented with light.

Accommodation Test Hold your penlight in front of the child's nose a couple of feet away. Bring the penlight toward the nose to see if the child's eyes move inward toward the nose.

Flashing Test Slowly shine the light in one eye, then the other, alternating from one eye to the other a few times. Check for pupil changes similar to the images below.

Regular   **Dilated**   **Contracted**

Vestibulo-ocular Reflex Test
1. Have the child look at a target, such as your penlight, a marker, or a sticker placed on a pencil.
2. Ask the child to look at the target while moving their head to maintain their gaze as the target is moved.
3. Move the target from left to right, up and down.
4. Observe the child's ability to maintain their gaze on the target. The eyes should move in the opposite direction of the head movement.
5. Repeat the previous steps and ask the child to not move their head while following the target with their eyes.
6. Observe the child's ability to maintain their gaze and follow the target without moving their head.

7.   Difficulties with any of the previous steps may indicate challenges with maintaining gaze, stabilizing eye movement with head positioning changes, and balance.

Part II: Heart and Respiratory Rate Have the child sit, and obtain their baseline breathing and heart rate. Avoid recording this information just after activities of high arousal or when the child is tired. Use the heart rate monitor device, if available, to gather the needed information. If you are using a stopwatch, obtain the pulse rate with the help of a knowledgeable professional. You can then use the stopwatch to record a 60-second interval, during which you should count the rises and falls of the child's chest during breathing.

Use the following chart as a guide for typical respiratory and heart rates. Being below or above the ranges may indicate the child's arousal level. If you desire, heart rate and respiratory recordings can be performed before and after attempted self-regulation activities. This information may provide additional information regarding the child's reaction to certain techniques.

TYPICAL RESPIRATORY AND HEART RATES IN CHILDREN		
Age (years)	**Breathing Rate** (per 60 seconds)	**Heart Rate** (per 60 seconds)
1–2	Approx. 22–37	98–140
3–5	20–28	80–120
6–11	18–25	75–118
12 and older	12–20	60–100
Adapted from Novak, C., & Gill, P., (2016). Pediatric vital signs reference chart. *PedsCases.com*. Retrieved from http://www.pedscases.com/ pediatric-vital-signs-reference-chart		

ANIMAL ASSESSMENTS
FOR LITTLE ONES

AIM To help identify the child's typical arousal and threshold level

POSITION AND ENVIRONMENT Well-lit room with an open area in which to move around

To start, you will need to describe the following animals and their characteristics

- Kangaroo: Likes to hop around and move and go on adventures
- Armadillo: Moves quickly and does not like to be touched or loud noises; it protects itself from other animals and things that are around it
- Hippopotamus: Moves slowly and is sometimes clumsy

PART I

Ask the child the following questions, then have them act like the animal discussed. Clarify the appropriate movement if they do not do it correctly.

1. How do you think a kangaroo moves? Show me (i.e., hopping around).

2. Do you know what an armadillo looks like? How do they protect themselves? Show me (i.e., balling their body up on the floor).

3. What does a hippopotamus look like, and how does it move? Show me (i.e., walking around slowly).

PART II

Ask the child the following questions

1. Which animal are you most like? Or, are you not like any of the animals we discussed?

2. Would you like to be a different animal? Which one?

Look for challenges in the child's movement or willingness to participate. The verbal and observable information shared may indicate their sensory preferences. "Kangaroos" may have high arousal levels and crave movement and a lot of self-initiated sensory input. "Armadillos" may be overresponsive and avoid sensory input and dislike engagement. Their arousal may be high, but their threshold is low. The "hippopotamus" may have challenges moving and avoid or have challenges with physical activity, handwriting, and self-help tasks. Their arousal and threshold levels may vary.

ASSESSMENT FOR NONVERBAL CHILDREN

AIM To help identify the child's typical arousal level in addition to sensory preferences

The following are important factors to keep in mind and ways to prepare before beginning the assessment:

1. Acknowledge the level of the child on the **Self-Regulation and Mindfulness 7-Level Hierarchy.** If the child is at the **foundational level,** you may need to obtain the following information through observation or caregiver interview rather than through active assessment activities. Printouts can be provided to the teacher or parent.

2. Observe the child during activities of low arousal, such as sitting in class, playing with peers, or eating at the table.

3. Make playing cards by printing images of activities of low arousal, such as sitting in class, playing with peers, eating at the table, sleeping, receiving a massage, or sitting on a bean bag chair.

4. Observe the child during activities of high arousal, such as playing on the playground, engaging in gym activities, or taking movement breaks (breaks from other activities to allow the child to engage in a variety of fast, slow, and cross-lateral movements).

5. Print pictures of activities of high arousal, such as swinging, jumping on a trampoline, dancing, or riding a bike or scooter board.

6. Observe the child during eating. Present them with various food types, such as bland, sweet, spicy, chewy, or crunchy.

7. Print images displaying food types, such as bland starches, sweets, bitter/sour foods, spicy foods, chewy foods, or crunchy foods.

8. Obtain a CD player or smartphone to play music. You will need different forms of music, such as classical, ambient, heavy metal, or rhythmic pop.

9. Gather items of different temperatures, such as ice cubes or heating pads.

10. Please note: These activities most likely will require more than one session. It is preferable to present them in short segments and repeat them on different days. This may assist in gaining a better picture of the child's overall arousal level versus just getting a "snapshot."

POSITION AND ENVIRONMENT Can vary

Observe the child in the various scenarios identified in the previous list. Record your observations. Organize an interview with the teacher and/or parent(s). Obtain as much information as possible from those individuals. Have a session with the child, and present them with various sensory stimuli or items described in the previous list. Take note of their responses.

If appropriate, review with the child familiar phrases, such as "I want" or "Give me," or gestures, such as shaking their head "yes" or "no." Then, work with the child using your selected method and make note of what they prefer; for example, show them cards depicting low- or high-arousal activities and ask them to gesture "yes" or "no" to show which they like better. You can then use a similar process to assess their preferences for stimuli such as music and temperature. Develop a sensory chart similar to the one provided on the next page to record your findings.

Work with your team to provide preferred stimuli to the child while also attempting to present some non-preferred stimuli to build flexibility. Remember that children will use behaviors and seek stimuli that they believe work best. They may rely primarily on one system, such as movement or proprioception, to block out undesired stimulation. The things they prefer provide comfort. While those items may be useful, we need to be sure to present novel items in a nonthreatening fashion to expand the child's repertoire. The activities for the various targets outlined in later chapters can be helpful in this process. You may find it helpful to complete a chart such as the following to record the child's sensory preferences.

SENSORY STIMULATION PREFERENCES			
	Notes	Yes	No
Movement			
Food			
Music			
Temperature			

WATER ASSESSMENT

AIM To help identify the child's typical threshold and arousal levels and stimuli supporting or impeding their function

YOU WILL NEED

- To select the environment (i.e., home or school) about which you will ask the child during the activity
- 5 disposable cups
- Marker
- A container of water
- Food coloring (optional)
- Measuring cup or large cup

POSITION AND ENVIRONMENT At a tabletop or flat surface in a well-lit room

PART I

Use the marker to label levels on each of the five cups with "Okay," "A lot," and "Too much" and to mark the large cup or measuring cup with "My arousal." Make three lines on the large cup labeled "Low," "Medium," "High". Provide the child with water, which can be clear or colored with food coloring. Read the child the following questions and ask them to pour water into each cup to reflect their answer. (You can select your own questions or modify the ones provided as needed.)

1. In your classroom (or at home) describe the noise.
2. Describe the lighting in your classroom (or at home).

3. Describe how comfortable the chairs are in your classroom (or at home): Are they okay, pretty uncomfortable ("A lot"), or very uncomfortable ("Too much")?

4. Describe the smells in your classroom (or at home).

5. Describe the sitting time (length of time you have to sit in a chair) at school (or at home).

Have the child pour the water from each cup onto the large cup (or measuring cup) labeled "My arousal" and see what level the water reaches ("Low," "Medium," or "High").

PART II

Now, write "A little," "Somewhere in the middle," and "A lot" on the five cups (or on new cups if the previously used ones cannot be reused), and ask the child the next set of questions, having them pour water into the cups again. As before, these questions can be modified if needed.

1. How much noise do you prefer?

2. How much light do you prefer?

3. How long do you like to sit?

4. How much do you like to smell things?

5. How soft of a seat do you like to sit on?

Relabel the large cup (or measuring cup) with "My threshold" (or use a new cup if the previously used one cannot be reused). Pour the water from the five cups into the large cup and see whether the water reaches "Low", "Medium," or "High."

Talk with the child about the differences between what they like and dislike and what they experience in the various situations that relate to the questions. Have the child use the **SAM box radio dial** on page 42 to illustrate how they feel ("Quiet," "Middle," or "Loud") when they experience the items presented in the questions. This information helps indicate the child's threshold and arousal level. Such details can inform you when you are selecting target activities provided in this program.

WHAT PLANT ARE YOU?

AIM To help identify the child's typical arousal level and methods to support sensory needs

YOU WILL NEED

- To have the child complete the water assessment
- To discuss with the child what plant is more like them (i.e., orchid, fern, cactus or aloe plant)
- To obtain the plant (optional)

POSITION AND ENVIRONMENT Can vary

PART I

Are you a(n) … ?

1. Orchid—particular about the amount of water and light needed; may need the support of a stick to hold it up; needs a lot of care
2. Fern—needs lots of water, humidity, space to move; needs medium level of support to thrive
3. Cactus or aloe plant—survives in most conditions with small amount of care

ASK THE CHILD TO DISCUSS THE FOLLOWING

- How would you care for your plant?
- Discuss what they need every day.
- What do you need every day?
- If you are not getting enough of what you need, how can you fix that?
- What are some things you can do in school or at home?

Refer to the target activities of this program.

PART II

Optional Mindfulness Component

While caring for your plant, simply care for your plant. You can talk to the plant but not to others in that moment. Try focusing on your plant and nothing else! Be mindful of how you care for it. This is a daily exercise that should be practiced consistently.

BONUS Compare the child's results with your own! How are you similar? How are you different? How do you think this affects your interactions with the child? What changes can you make?

METRONOME ASSESSMENT

AIM To help identify the child's typical arousal and threshold levels to inform methods to enhance self-regulation

YOU WILL NEED

- To select the environment (i.e., home or school) about which you will ask the child during the activity
- A metronome or a metronome app on your electronic device (which can be obtained for free in most cases)

POSITION AND ENVIRONMENT Well-lit room

PART I

Choose an environment to discuss (e.g., home, school, playground) as well as specific scenarios. You can choose scenarios such as bedtime, sitting in class, or going to the playground. Review how the child normally feels in those environments. Ask them questions relating to the following elements of the scenarios chosen:

1. How does noise make you feel?
2. How does light in the space make you feel?
3. How do you feel when you are sitting?
4. How do you feel when you are moving?
5. How much do you like to smell things?

PART II

Show the child that a fast-moving metronome can be an example of how our bodies feel when we are not comfortable or became nervous or scared. Then, show them that a slow-moving metronome is similar to how our bodies feel when we are tired or bored. Use the metronome to have them represent how they typically feel in those environments and scenarios. Review the obtained information regarding their arousal to select target activities within this program.

OLDER CHILD SELF-ASSESSMENT

AIM To help identify the child's typical arousal and threshold level and teach them about their sensory preferences supporting or impeding daily function

YOU WILL NEED
- A pencil and paper (optional)
- List of provided questions

POSITION AND ENVIRONMENT Any environment that is comfortable for the child

PART I

Ask the child to complete the list of inquiries on page 58. Follow with a discussion about how certain environments and sensory stimuli can help us get through our day or make it challenging. Explore how the child can use that knowledge. Lastly, use the information gathered to select among the daily target activities that are provided in later chapters.

SELF-ASSESSMENT

1. I would best describe myself as: (circle all that apply)

    a) Enjoying a lot of activity (e.g., movement, running, jumping)
    b) Avoiding physical activity
    c) Being a thrill-seeker (e.g., enjoying climbing)
    d) Disliking loud or irritating sounds (e.g., other people talking)
    e) Disliking certain lighting, such as the lights at school
    f) Preferring to wear only one type of clothing (e.g., sweatpants)

2. I would describe my eating and appetite as follows: (circle all that apply)

    a) Sometimes I have difficulty knowing when I am hungry until the last minute.
    b) I am always hungry and/or thirsty.
    c) I only like certain foods and am somewhat picky.

3. I would describe my bodily functions as follows: (circle all that apply)

    a) I often have to use the bathroom and have to rush to get there in time.
    b) I do not have to use the bathroom often.
    c) I do not like using the bathroom (because _____).
    d) I often feel my heart racing.
    e) I often breathe quickly or heavily.
    f) I do not feel my heart race or breathe quickly.
    g) I do not like a lot of movement.

4. I am a daydreamer (e.g., my thoughts drift off in class). Circle Yes or No

5. What bothers me the most while in class is:

6. What bothers me the most while in public is:

7. What makes me feel better when I am upset, said, or irritated is:

chapter 5

Lessons on the Four Principles

It is important for children to understand their sensory experiences. It is just as important that they learn how to recognize and accept their emotions. This chapter talks about how our environment and events around us lead to our behavior. We explore how emotions can support us or stand in our way.

Children should not be taught to avoid their emotions but rather recognize the feelings that arise through their senses. Doing so provides an opportunity for them to learn to use appropriate responses rather than spontaneous reactions. Lastly, this chapter reviews how mindfulness facilitates executive functioning in addressing self-regulation. It is necessary to acknowledge that some children who are at the foundational level of our **Self-Regulation and Mindfulness 7-Level Hierarchy** will have challenges understanding the lessons in this chapter. In these situations, it is the adult's job to gain an understanding of these concepts, which will allow them to accept and further understand the behaviors of the child. When the adult can do so, reciprocal regulation and mindfulness come into play.

The lessons learned should be applied to the adult's own emotions that arise in the presence of challenging behaviors of the child. Even children at the foundational level can benefit and make improvements when the daily target activities are implemented. Use your judgment when deciding with whom to share the following lessons. **Most parents and caregivers should find the information easy to follow. However, if the delivery seems too complex for some, feel free to use the "Short SAM Stories" to help further explain the concepts.**

1. Multisensory Integration
2. Emotional Regulation
3. Executive Functioning and Mindfulness
4. Mindfulness and Compassion

MULTISENSORY INTEGRATION LESSONS

Lesson #1: What Is Our Sensory System?

Our senses allow us to connect to our surroundings. They include touch, taste, sound, sight, smell, movement, and balance. We also have senses that arise from inside of our bodies. Together, all of these senses make up our sensory system. Senses are important to our safety and allow us to gain an understanding of our surroundings. For example, they tell us how the weather feels, the taste of food, and whether a song has a good beat for dancing. Sometimes we like what we feel, and our feelings make it easier for us to do what we need to do. However, our feelings can also take over our bodies and make it hard for us to listen and follow directions. For example, you may like to run, climb, and jump, but sitting still to listen to your teacher in class may be challenging. Or, you may not like how certain clothing feels on your body but enjoy a big bear hug from a family member.

Sometimes our sensory system goes into overdrive: A fast heartbeat, heavy breathing, sweaty hands, and feelings of excitement or nervousness are examples of times when it feels like your senses are taking over. You may want to stop and leave the activity you are doing, or you can become so excited you have difficulty listening to your parent, teacher, or friends. This happens when your body lets too much sensory information enter into your brain. Just like trains traveling along the tracks, messages from your senses travel through your body. They begin their trip at a starting point and then travel along to their destination.

Think of your senses as trains trying to enter into your "train station," your brain. Before a train can arrive at the station, it needs permission from a guard to enter safely. Similarly, before the messages from your senses can reach your brain, they have to get permission to enter. Your "guard" will either allow or stop them from coming into the station. If your guard does a good job, your body feels good. When your guard does not do a good job, too much information will come through, making you feel uncomfortable. It is your responsibility to get your guard to work correctly, to do so, you must practice "exercising your senses."

Just like our muscles, our senses need exercise. Activities that excite your sensory system give you power. It is important to exercise all of your senses! When the senses work together, they are your super power! When your senses are working together well, we call that multisensory integration. Using more than one sense at the same time at the same place makes all of your sensory powers stronger. This requires you to explore and try new things. You may be surprised to discover what it's like to try new things and build your sensory system's power.

Short SAM Story: Millie the Armadillo

Millie is an armadillo who liked to roam around the rainforest. Millie enjoyed playing by herself. She did not like it when the other armadillos ran and bumped into her. Millie also did not like all the loud noises they would make. When others came around, she would hide in her shell and ball up. Sometimes, Millie would push others away when they got too close.

When she was alone, Millie loved to roll around and eat her favorite yummy foods. But, she did not realize what she was missing: While Millie enjoyed rolling around and eating, she was missing out on having friends and learning new things.

One day, Millie's mother had a surprise for her: She was sending Millie to camp. Well, Millie was not happy and frankly became scared. She began to cry and hide. Her mother said, "Millie, I am sorry, but I think this will be good for you. You will have fun!"

The next day, Millie arrived at camp. There, she met her counselors, who would care for the campers and lead them in activities each day. The counselors shared that camp would involve a variety of activities, such as swimming, hiking, and camping. This did not sound like fun to Millie! She felt her heart beating fast and began to breathe deeply. Her skin became sweaty, and Millie wanted to get away. Before she could go into her shell to hide, one counselor named Sarah came over and said hello. "What's your name?" asked Sarah. Millie shared her name, and Sarah introduced herself. "You seem a little nervous," said Sarah. "I was also scared when I first got here. Give it a chance!"

That night, Millie went to her cabin. To her surprise, Sarah was there as well. While this made Millie happy, she soon realized that the cabin was cold and uncomfortable. Sarah noticed that Millie seemed sad. She asked Millie if she wanted a sleeping bag. This was something Millie never heard of before, but she was cold and decided to give it a try. Millie crawled inside and realized that it was very comfy. It was soft, and she loved how heavy it felt on her shell. Sarah also allowed Millie to borrow an mp3 player with a pair of headphones so she could listen to soothing music. After a good night's sleep, Millie was curious to see what the morning would bring.

First was breakfast. Nothing looked good! However, Millie thought about how she had been willing to try using the sleeping bag and figured she would try something to eat, too. She usually enjoyed soft and chewy food. There was a piece of toast and some applesauce. Millie decided to dip the toast into the applesauce to soften the bread. Surprisingly, it was not bad!

Later, Sarah sat with Millie to have a talk. She told Millie that she wanted to teach her something. Sarah told her about the "senses." "Sometimes we like the things around us, like smells or things we touch or tastes," said Sarah. "But sometimes we do not like them. When we do not like things we sense, or if we get too much sensory information at once, our bodies can feel yucky. That is when your heart races or your breathing gets heavy. Sometimes, your skin can get sweaty."

"What can I do about my senses?" asked Millie. "You can first say hello to those feelings," said Sarah. You don't have to say it aloud, but simply know that the feelings are there. Then, you can stop them from taking over. Take a deep breath or do something else that feels good, like giving yourself a big squeeze. But first you need to make your senses stronger and exercise them by trying new things. Try to use more than one sense at a time, like listening to music while doing yoga." Millie thanked Sarah and told her she would give it a shot. "Hmm," thought Millie. "Maybe I *should* give new things a try." From that day, she decided to try and have fun at camp. Sometimes things seemed scary, or she tried something and did not like it after all. But Millie felt stronger.

When Millie returned home from camp, things were different. Millie noticed how beautiful the trees looked. She also realized that the other children seemed to be having lots of fun playing and exploring. Millie thought about how much she missed out on before going to camp. She also remembered that maybe she had not been so nice at times. When she had hidden in her shell or pushed the other children, they may have thought she was mean.

As Millie began to think about the past, she started feeling her heart racing and her skin getting sweaty. She then noticed that those were signs that her senses were trying to take over. Millie remembered what Sarah had told her and took a deep breath. Instead of hiding in her shell or pushing others away, Millie walked over to the playground. Before she knew it, a new friend came and invited her to play. Millie realized that she had exercised her senses and was indeed stronger!

The End

After reading the story, ask the children what they learned from it. Ask them to try and explain what the senses are. What are signs that your senses are taking over? How can you use your senses to be more successful? Use the story to talk through how we can strengthen our sensory system. What are some of the strategies Millie used to calm her senses? How the children sometimes feel when presented with certain smells, tastes, sounds, sights, touch, or movements.

EMOTIONAL REGULATION LESSON

Lesson #2: What Are Emotions?

Emotions are the result of feelings that lead to a reaction. When something happens to us, good or bad, our bodies feel a change. The change can feel "yucky" or kind of nice. When you become upset, you may feel your heart beat fast and your face, lips, and cheeks become tight. You may breathe quickly, and your arms and legs become tense. Even your stomach may feel sort of strange. When something good happens, you may feel your body become calm. Your face may still change: Your lips may relax, and your cheeks may rise. The funny thing about our emotions is that they can be very strong, but they are not so smart.

Strong emotions can take over your brain and tell it what to do. However, each of your emotions only knows one thing! Fear only knows how to be fearful. Frustration only knows how to be frustrated. An emotion can confuse us and only allow us to look, think, and act in one way. If you become angry, your emotions only allow you to think, look, and talk angrily. When you feel sad, the sad emotions only let you think about sadness. The same goes for emotions like joy: When you have joy, you think and feel joyful!

All emotions can cause you to do something without thinking. You may want to throw something when you are angry. You may want to hug someone when you have joy. These are called **reactions**. Even though each of our emotions only knows one thing, we have different emotions that take turns in our brain. You cannot change an emotion. For example, anger does not just turn into happiness. However, you can stop the emotion from telling you how to think.

You can stop yourself from having a quick reaction, so that you can decide on your actions. The emotion gets weaker, and you become stronger! You can **respond instead of react**! When you decide to respond, or do something that is not controlled by the emotion, new feelings may occur. If you were sad, doing something fun or thinking about someone you love can cause you to feel happier. Your face may change into a smile. Then, your body introduces a new feeling, joy.

Introduction to the FADS and JEL Feelings

There are a number of different emotions, and feelings connected to those emotions. It is hard to say how many exist. However, there are a few strong feelings that are likely to arise in our bodies more often than other ones. Trying to understand these more common feelings can help us choose to have better responses to our emotions. We are going to learn about two groups of feelings. The first is called **FADS**: Frustration, Anxiety, Desire, and Sadness.

The **F** (for **Frustration**) is when your body and face become tense. Your heart races, and your breathing is heavy. You may want to quit doing what you're doing or hit something. These feelings may remind you of being angry.

The **A** (for **Anxiety**) causes you to worry, and your stomach may feel funny. Some may call that sensation "having butterflies in your stomach." You may want to hide and avoid what is causing the feeling. You may have felt like this when afraid.

The **D** (for **Desire**) can lead to a fast heartbeat and being focused on one thing. You have trouble listening to or talking with others because you only want that one thing.

Lastly the **S** (for **Sadness**) can cause you to feel weak. You may want to ball up and cry. These feelings often make us feel confused and lonely.

All of the **FADS** cause strong reactions in our bodies. They can take over your thoughts and make things difficult for you. The good thing is FADS usually do not last long—at least if you do not allow them to take over. You should not feel ashamed when having FADS—these feelings are normal, and everyone has them sometimes. You just need to know how to not always react to them. Sometimes, FADS keep us out of harm. For example, when danger is near, you must listen to FADS to protect yourself. If a dangerous animal is near, your FADS alarm you to stay away!

The challenging part of having FADS is that they may last longer if you overreact. When you overreact, you can miss out on the good things happening around you. For example, if you allow FADS feelings to last too long, they can get in the way of a fun activity like going to play with friends. Reacting to FADS in certain ways can also cause someone else to have FADS. When that happens, your strong FADS feelings can last even longer. Once we know how to act or not react, the FADS will not last as long and may be replaced with new feelings.

The second group of feelings is **JEL** feelings: Joy, Enthusiasm, and Love. These feelings last longer than FADS and allow us to work better with others. Like FADS, your JEL feelings can lead to other people around you to have similar feelings. The difference is that JEL feelings are usually helpful and allow us to get along with others.

The **J** (for **Joy**) can cause your heart to flutter, your face to smile, and an overall good feeling to enter your body. This may be what you feel when you play or spend time with friends.

The **E** (for **Enthusiasm**) can lead to focusing on something you want or need while still being able to listen and talk with others. For example, this may involve being able to listen and follow the directions to earn a treat.

Last is **L** (for **Love**). When we feel love, we have a lot of good sensations in our body. We feel protected and want to be with other people. We also want other people to have those same feelings. You may experience this feeling with family or someone you care about. When JEL feelings replace FADS, they may help us do what we need to do and want to do in appropriate ways.

What Causes Your FADS?

Adults: If appropriate, explain each component of FADS—frustration (anger), anxiety (fear), desire (longing), and sadness (panic or discomfort) to the child. If explaining these concepts to the child is not appropriate (i.e., they are not at a developmental level to understand them), continue reading and/or read one of our Short SAM Stories.

FADS are the feelings that make us feel "yucky." They come quickly and are strong. There are a few things that can cause FADS. Your **senses** can cause them. For example, you may not like certain sounds, smells, touch, or tastes, and encountering these can cause FADS. What are some things that you do not like? Think about them. How do you feel? Even just thinking about those things can cause the "yucky" feelings. We may also have FADS feelings when we are surprised.

Not knowing when something will happen or what will come next can lead to feelings of shock or panic. Going to a new place and meeting new people are examples. There is another cause of FADS that may seem kind of strange: Things we like can also lead to FADS. For example, you may think about a thing you really like (e.g., a toy, food, running and playing) or try to get it *constantly*. It is okay to want the things that make us happy, but these wants can trigger FADS when they take over. They take us away from our responsibilities: You may stop doing your work, listening to the teacher, or playing nicely with friends just to get that thing you desire. When you are not able to get what you want, you may become upset, causing your body to not feel so good.

When you experience FADS, you may not like how your body feels. It can feel uncomfortable. Your brain does not like it when your body is tense and your heart races. Your brain likes to keep everything balanced and calm. So, when FADS occur, your brain will try to make you feel better. It will send out messengers—

chemicals that make your body feel good—to stop the unwanted feelings in the body. When this happens, even though you may start to feel better, it can be confusing. You may start seeking out experiences that cause FADS to get that good feeling again.

Unfortunately, the good feelings in these situations usually do not last long, causing you to want more and more. Even though you may want to do a good job, the FADS can then get in your way! Your body learns how to feel better for a short period of time by using FADS to get those feel-good chemicals from your brain, but you may get into a lot of trouble. If you are not careful, you may allow yourself to have more FADS than JEL feelings. This can cause problems because the good experiences we get with JEL feelings may be stronger and last for longer periods of time than those with the FADS.

How to Recognize FADS and JEL Feelings

Review the following pictures and see if you can act out the FADS and JEL feelings that are depicted. Play a game with two or three friends to see if you can guess the feeling they are acting out. If you have four or more friends nearby, you can form teams to play the game. You can also take a look in the mirror to play by yourself. How do your body and face look when you have certain feelings? Remember, it is okay to have any kind of feelings. but sometimes we want to learn ways for us to quiet our feelings when they become too loud. What are some of the things you can do?

First, let's review the FADS feelings and how to notice the signs.

1. **Frustration:** Fast heartbeat, sweaty palms, tense muscles, tight lips or open mouth, lower eyebrows

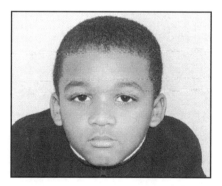

2. **Anxiety:** Fast heartbeat, heavy breathing, tight muscles, sweaty palms, flexed posture, raised eyebrows, widened eyes, tense or open mouth, moving a lot or attempting to hide, covering face or ears, arms and legs brought up close to the body

3.   **Desire:** Raised cheeks and eyebrows, fast heartbeat (sometimes), fixated eyes, lots of movement from excitement, difficulty listening and attending to others

4.   **Sadness:** Flexed body, arms close to the body, raised inner corner of the eyebrows, downward-slanted cheeks, pouting lips

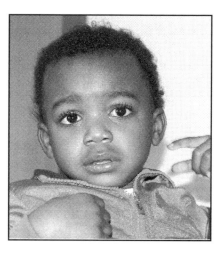

Now, let's review the JEL feelings.

1.   **Joy:** Smiling, separated teeth, calm breathing and heartbeat, raised cheeks, relaxed and comfortable body, bright eyes, extended neck, slightly tilted back head (sometimes)

2. **Enthusiasm:** Wide open eyes, tall trunk, extended arms and legs, slightly increased heartbeat, slightly raised eyebrows and cheeks, slightly turned up mouth corners

3. **Love:** Similar to joy and enthusiasm (feeling compassion toward someone else, relaxed body and face, lowered eyelids, head tilted to the side [sometimes], slightly raised corner of lips)

It takes practice to recognize the FADS and JEL feelings. Once you become better at spotting the signs, you will be more successful at interacting with others. Take time to read the SAM Story about Max the Kangaroo, which follows. It will help explain how we sometimes do not recognize the feelings that can stand in our way!

Short SAM Story: Max the Kangaroo

Max lived in a beautiful big open land. Every day, he played and explored. He loved jumping and bouncing all around. However, one day Max's mother told him he had to go to school. Max was scared. What was school? Even though his mother tried to tell him about it, he was still nervous and afraid. Finally, the day came for Max's first day at school. "Lots of rooms, desks, chairs, things, and people all around … I don't know about this!" thought Max.

He met his teacher who showed him his room and where to sit. Max sat at his desk. The chair felt weird, and the lights seemed strange. Max was used to playing in his open field in the beautiful bright sunlight. This all was odd to him, and he felt a little yucky. "Maybe if I stand, I will feel better," thought Max, so he stood up. But, his teacher quickly said, "Max, please have a seat!" Max sat down, but he still felt yucky. Max decided to lay his head down on the desk and cover his eyes. Soon after, his teacher came over to his desk. "Max, you need to listen to me teach. This is what we do at school," said his teacher.

Well, Max really felt confused and did not know what to do. He noticed that there was a window near his desk. He became excited. Outside of the window was a playground with swings and lots of fun-looking things. He wondered whether he could go outside. "I am going to swing all day," thought Max. He could not stop thinking about going outside. He didn't even hear his teacher tell him it was time to eat lunch. She had to call him three times before he got his lunch bag.

After lunch, Max was so happy to learn that he could go to the playground. He hopped quickly toward the swings. But, someone was in his way. Max kept hopping, with the swing on his mind, and bumped into another classmate. They both began to cry. Max had to go talk to his teacher and the principal. Now he was in trouble, AND he never got to swing! Max explained his day to the teacher and principal. He told them how he was afraid, felt yucky, and did not like the classroom. He also told them how he wanted to swing. They started telling Max about these things called *FADS*. Max learned that what he felt that day were FADS (frustration, anxiety, desire, and sadness)—feelings that can take over your brain and make you feel strange. These feelings are powerful and try to control your body. Max learned that the best way to feel better is to know when the FADS are around.

Max learned that his stomach may feel funny, his heart may beat fast, and his body feels strange when FADS happen. When FADS take over, you start to think about ways to feel better. You may have trouble listening to or seeing the people around you. When that happens, you may break the rules, and others can get hurt like the kid Max had bumped into.

Max also learned that there are a few things you can do about FADS. The first thing he learned was to tell an adult, such as his mother or teacher. At school, his teacher would be able to tell him a few ways he could feel better without breaking the rules. The teacher showed Max how to "blow out" the FADS like candles on a birthday cake. Then, she showed him how to do push-ups on the wall and dips on his chair. Max's muscles were working hard!

After practicing some exercises with his teacher, Max did feel better! He learned that FADS are not necessarily bad, as long as he did not let them take over! He was in charge. His teacher told him that noticing the FADS and taking a break to do an activity that helped could lead him to JEL feelings (joy, enthusiasm, and love), which cause our bodies to feel good and help us to get stronger over time. "When those FAD feelings sneak in, be sure to notice them so they won't hang around too long!" said his teacher. "Then welcome the JEL feelings. We want them to stick around."

Max ended up having a great first day at school. He could not wait to go home and tell his mother all about FADS and teach her some of the exercises his teacher taught him.

The End

After reading the story, ask the children what they learned from it. Ask them to try and explain FADS and JEL feelings and identify FADS using the specific examples from Max's story. You can then select one of the target activities. Tell the children that the activity was one that Max learned from his teacher. How do they feel during and after the activity?

Lesson #3: Executive Functioning and Mindfulness

The large front part of our brain allows us to be in control. We get stronger when the front part of our brain is in charge of the emotional brain areas. Despite what we feel from our senses and the emotions that come about, we can still be in control. You can notice and accept your feelings and emotions. It is okay and actually healthy to have emotions, even FADS. Your job is to not let FADS sneak in and take over. When FADS feelings are too loud, we have a hard time hearing and seeing the important things around us. Luckily, the front part of our brain is the "leader." Let it lead!

We can solve many problems when we allow our "leader," the front part of our brain, to make decisions and offer different ideas for us to choose. Sometimes things will not work as planned. In those cases, it is up to our leader to help us change and work with new situations that arise. Most importantly, the front part of the brain allows us to stop doing something! Before you let your emotions take control or do something that is not so nice, you have the power to stop. When we stop, our brain is able to come up with a better idea rather than our doing something negative. These abilities get stronger when we are more aware of the present moment.

Here is a way you can practice: Stop and take a second to look around. What colors do you see? How does the air feel on your skin? Who is nearby? How does your body feel? Now, did you notice anything else? Perhaps stopping to pay attention to what is happening in the present made it harder to think about something that previously made you upset. Maybe you did not think about what was going to happen later on in the day. You just experienced **mindfulness**. Being mindful is being present. Being present is a gift because it helps us to slow down and notice things.

The great thing about mindfulness activities is that they allow our brain to get exercise. Not only does our leader get stronger, so does the part of the brain we call the "teacher"—the IC (insular cortex), which is near the emotional parts of our brain. It works with both of those areas to teach them right from wrong. When we stop and pay attention, take a deep breath, and explore our senses, the teacher is at work! If our emotions lead us to make a poor choice, the teacher will send a message to our body that will not feel so good; the purpose of this process is to help us avoid repeating the poor choice that caused us not to feel good. However, if we are doing well, making good decisions, the teacher will let us know that as well. The message sent to our body in these cases will feel great! The IC helps to teach the body and mind to connect so that we get better at **self-regulation**, having more control over our feelings and actions.

Read the SAM Story that follows about the garden. It teaches us how mindfulness can help our brain get stronger. When our brain gets exercise, we are able to do better. It can also lead us to joy, enthusiasm, and love!

Short SAM Story: The Garden

Jackson lived in a big city. There were always a lot of people, loud noises, and things happening all around. Jackson did not mind living in the city. but sometimes it all seemed like too much. For example, Jackson's mom would ride with him on the city bus to school. Riding the bus was sometimes frustrating for Jackson. People would bump into him and knock into his book bag. Some would step on his feet without saying they were sorry! Being in school was not much different for Jackson. His school had both small and big kids. The big kids would move quickly and not see the smaller kids like him. Jackson spent most of the morning trying to keep up and avoid being run over.

One morning, Jackson told his mother he was not feeling well. She took his temperature and seemed confused. "Jackson, you do not have a fever," she said. "You seem okay to me. What is wrong?" Jackson looked away and did not speak. After his mother continued to ask, he finally exclaimed, "I hate going to school! I also hate that bus! I wish I could stay home forever!" His mother was shocked. "I always thought you enjoyed school," she said. "I am sure you are just having a bad day. Let's get ready to go and talk about this later."

That day, Jackson tried to enjoy himself. He wanted to have a good time at school and decided to give it a try. That was until he got to the playground! As he attempted to climb up the sliding board, another kid ran past him, pushing him out of the way. Jackson ran over to give the kid a big shove. In that moment, he felt someone come up from behind. It was his teacher, Mr. Johnson. Mr. Johnson walked Jackson inside to have a talk. He told Jackson that he would have to call his mother and share what happened at recess. Jackson said, "So what! I don't care!"

Mr. Johnson said, "Jackson, even though you are saying that, I think that you do care. If you did not care, you would not have done anything. You would have not pushed your classmate." "Well he pushed me first!" exclaimed Jackson. Mr. Johnson shared that he understood, but said, "Even when something like that happens, we do not have to react. There is a difference between reacting and responding." Jackson looked confused. "Let me show you," said Mr. Johnson.

Mr. Johnson walked Jackson over to the science station in the classroom, where there was an indoor garden. "You see this garden?" said Mr. Johnson to Jackson. "It took a lot of work to get the vegetables to grow inside. I failed many times." Mr. Johnson pulled out a photo album sitting nearby. "I took these pictures to show you all what the garden looked like from when it started to now." Jackson was surprised to see dirt and dead plants in some of the photos in the book. He could not believe that was the same garden. "But what does this have to do with me?" asked Jackson.

"Well, I got frustrated, anxious, and even sad trying to get the plants to grow," said Mr. Johnson. "I had so much desire to make the garden succeed that I stopped enjoying the act of gardening. I wanted to take the whole thing and throw it in the trash can. Instead of reacting, I decided to stop and take a break. I remembered why I liked to garden. The smell and feel of the soil made me smile. I loved watching the seeds sprout and grow into a plant. When I stopped my reaction, I was able to come up with an idea! I would change the location and the soil and keep trying, even if it did not work out again! You have the same choice!"

Mr. Johnson told Jackson that he always had the option to stop and think. Stopping a reaction allows for a response! Responses are better, because we choose them rather than allowing our emotions to tell us how to react. The front part of our brain then takes over, which allows us to be strong and to tell the emotional brain who is in charge! Mr. Johnson shared that we can practice responding by becoming more aware of what is going on around us. We can be mindful. Being mindful is being present. Being present is a gift! That is when we do our best work!

Mr. Johnson explained to Jackson that there is a small area in the brain that teaches us what it feels like to make good or not-so-good decisions. "When you react, the teacher will not be happy, and your body may feel yucky," said Mr. Johnson. "When you choose to have a response and the front part of your brain becomes the leader, the teacher is happy! Your body learns and grows when you are more aware of the moment. Your brain is very powerful! But, you first must pay attention." Mr. Johnson then had an idea. "You should grow your own garden!" he said to Jackson. "When I speak with your mother, I will tell her about our plan to work on you responding and being more mindful."

Mr. Johnson gathered some of his extra supplies and some seeds from the back. When Jackson's mother arrived at school, Mr. Johnson shared the details about the garden. Jackson took everything for the garden home. He was excited but nervous. What if he failed? Jackson then remembered how Mr. Johnson's plants died on his first try. Maybe it would not be so bad if his died as well. Jackson figured he would try anyway.

Day after day, Jackson cared for his plants. Mr. Johnson told him what to do and checked in with him every day. Jackson would tell him how the plants were doing. He loved planting the seeds in the soil and watching them sprout. Jackson could not believe that there were actual plants growing! Even his mom enjoyed watching the garden. Sometimes, Jackson and his mother could spend an hour looking at and talking about the garden.

One day, Jackson came home from school to find small, round vegetables growing from his plants. "Tomatoes!" yelled Jackson. His mom ran into his room. They both began to jump up and down with joy. Jackson had done it! He had grown a garden. He could not wait to return to school the next day to tell Mr. Johnson. As he shared his story, Mr. Johnson smiled. He reminded Jackson that the only way the garden had grown was because Jackson was present in the moment caring for the plants. And then … there was a gift—the tomatoes.

"You are strong, Jackson. You can do great things and control your brain to make decisions. You, my friend, know how to be mindful! I want you to remember that every day. Even if someone runs and pushes you out of the way, you can choose what to do. If you do not make the best decision, you could miss out on something good! Like your tomatoes!"

The End

After reading the story, ask the children what they learned from it. Ask them to try and explain mindfulness. Talk about the concepts of paying attention, listening to the "teacher," and allowing the front part of the brain to be the "leader." What is the role of the front part of the brain versus the emotional part of the brain? Then, identify the difference between reacting and responding. Ask for the children to provide specific examples from the story.

Lesson #4: Mindfulness and Compassion

Mindfulness requires us to be aware of what is happening in the present moment. We can then choose the best response. To make the best choice, we must be mindful of the needs of others and of ourselves. We must be compassionate to others and to ourselves. When we understand that our actions can affect other people, compassion begins. It is natural for humans to interact with other people.

Our bodies feel good when we are around others and we experience JEL feelings. Yet, when we experience the FADS of frustration, anxiety, desire, and sadness, we try to protect ourselves to feel better. We may not realize that while trying to make ourselves feel better, we may cause others around us to suffer.

It is okay to dislike something that someone has done to you. You should acknowledge that it was not something you appreciated. Yet, you must try to forgive the other person. This helps you to become more compassionate. While our emotions are strong and happen automatically, compassion is something we have to nurture. We have to remember to think about others.

When our emotions arise, we are sometimes not aware that they are there and may not be aware of how our actions are affecting others. If we try our best to always think about how our actions can affect other people and how they may help or harm ourselves, we become more aware. If I do not listen to the teacher, what will happen? Will I have to leave the activity? Will she become frustrated? If I let my sister have a turn on the game, will it bring her joy? Will she show me love? Everything we do can cause FADS or JEL feelings for us and the people around us. The more JEL feelings we have, the more others may have, and the cycle continues. Compassion can lead us to have a more fulfilling life.

Read the following SAM Story about Harry the Hippopotamus. It teaches us how compassion can make things easier. The story also shows us how our actions can either help someone else or cause them to have FADS.

Short SAM Story: Harry the Hippopotamus

Harry the Hippopotamus did not have many friends. He would go to school, eat lunch alone, then come home and play inside. It wasn't that Harry did not want friends: The other kids did not want to play with him. Harry was not fast. When all the children would go to gym, no one wanted to be on Harry's team for fear of losing the game. During recess, Harry would accidently bump into others because of his large size. In class, he tried his best but would work very slowly. His teacher would ask him to speed up to finish his assignments, but, Harry just could not work fast enough.

One day, Harry was in the cafeteria carrying his lunch to the table. He sat down, and the other children at the table stood up and walked away. Harry instantly became sad. Before he knew it, he was crying. A lunch aide came over to Harry and asked what was bothering him. Harry could not speak. She asked if it was because of the other children leaving the table. Harry shook his head "yes."

After lunch, the lunch aide walked Harry to his classroom. She spoke with his teacher and explained what happened. His teacher decided it was time to teach the class about compassion. "Compassion?" asked Harry. "Yes, compassion is thinking about others," said the teacher. "It is also thinking about ourselves and knowing how what we do will always lead to something. We want that something to be good!"

Once recess was over, all of the children returned to the classroom to find Harry and the teacher. In front of them was a fish in a bowl. "We have a new friend joining us today," said Harry's teacher. "The librarian is letting us keep her fish for the next couple of weeks. It is up to us to care for him." The children were very excited. They all tried to get closer and asked if they could feed the fish. The teacher explained that everyone would get a turn caring for the fish. Harry would be first. She then explained that caring for a fish requires more than just feeding it fish food.

"You have to clean the tank, talk to the fish, and be sure you do not forget to feed it three times a day," said Harry's teacher. "So, I must know that you are ready to handle the fish before giving you the job. You must show me compassion." All of the children looked confused except for Harry. She then asked Harry to explain what he had learned while the other children were at recess. Harry told the kids how we must think about others and how our actions will lead to something good or bad. If we do not think about the fish and doing everything it needs, it could get sick, but if we keep the fish in our thoughts, it may do well and be happy.

The teacher explained that she must see them thinking about others in the same way. She told them she would be watching to see who helped another classmate. "If I see you making someone smile, I will know that you are starting to understand what it means to be compassionate. But, if I see others becoming sad or upset because you are not being kind, I will know you need more time before you are able to care for the fish." That week, the children all worked hard to earn the job of caring for the fish. They even invited Harry to sit with them at lunch. In gym class, they did not seem to mind if Harry was on their team. They all just seemed excited to play and run around.

Everyone had a turn feeding the fish while it was with the class. After the fish was returned to the librarian, all the children had a better understanding of compassion. Harry's teacher decided to continue the lesson on compassion by buying everyone a small plant to care for as part of science class. She knew the lesson of compassion was powerful!

The End

After reading the story, ask the children what they learned from it. Ask them to try and explain compassion. Then, identify how not being compassionate could affect others. Ask for the children to provide specific examples from the story.

A Note on Reciprocal Regulation

Can you recall working with a child who became upset, did not want to participate, and displayed challenging behaviors? How did that make you feel? Close your eyes and imagine how your heart, breathing, skin, body, and face felt. Did you feel relaxed? It is my assumption that you recalled a moment when you felt stress or discomfort. We experience physical reactions based on someone else's behavior. If they smile at us, we may feel happy. If they frown at us, we can feel uncomfortable. When those around us are experiencing stress, we can as well.

Similarly, we must acknowledge our effect on others. When you approach a child who is upset when you also are tense and feeling stress, it can create a vicious cycle. Adults (and peers) trying to assist a child must take a moment to acknowledge their arousal levels. If your heart is racing and you feel tension in your body, take a moment to acknowledge the feelings. Then, take a breath or try another technique to relax your body. This is especially important when physically trying to calm a child. As you place your body near theirs, you are transferring your energy and arousal. Be mindful of your unconscious influence. Reciprocal regulation can be a support or hindrance to your interaction.

THE PRINCIPLES IN SUMMARY

Our Senses: First We Feel!

First, you feel. What you do with those feelings depends on your ability to stop automatic reactions and respond. Notice if your body changes. Do you feel your face and body getting tense, your heart speeding up, your palms getting sweaty? Say hello (to the feeling), stop, and then respond! Sometimes, we may need to ask for help in making the best choice. We may need something to help soothe our senses, such as big squeeze, quiet time alone, a movement break, or a drink of water. Other times, we may need someone else to help us! Use some time to give your body what it needs. A "SAM Pass" is a great way to request a break. (See an example in Chapter 6.)

Emotional Regulation: Be Mindful of Your Emotions!

Some emotions try to take over your brain. Some disguise themselves and need revealing so that you can move past the feeling! Letting the FADS feelings take over may lead you to miss out on something good. You are more successful when your long-term JEL feelings come into play. Remember, FADS (Frustration, Anxiousness, Desire, and Sadness) are strong feelings and can get in the way. JEL (Joy, Enthusiasm, and Love) feelings can help you get along well with others and do well! You have the power to be in control! You are stronger than your emotions. Everyone has a superhero within! Exercise your super power with daily experiences of FADS and JEL moments. We review these ideas in Chapter 7, where we describe the nine daily targets.

Executive Functioning and Mindfulness: Feel, See, and Be!

Children naturally live in the moment. However, in today's society, there are lots of stimuli occurring at once. Sometimes, a child being able to experience one moment at a time is helpful—just to feel, see, and be in tune with what is happening now. Being present can actually change our brain and improve our interactions! Breathing activities, meditation, and caring for others or plants allow us to be aware of the moment. The present is a gift. We must slow down to receive what the present has to offer. Use a "SAM Present" as a reminder. (See Chapter 6 for more details.)

EVERYDAY SAM PRACTICES

The following are important to incorporate into daily practice:

1. **Breath Breaks:** Take a moment to blow out the energy that builds up in your body. Sometimes, the energy comes from being busy, stressed, or upset. When we blow it out, we feel and work better. Parents, try taking 3 to 5 minutes at home before school for a Breath Break for you and your child. Teachers, take a short Breath Break before class begins and take Breath Breaks for you and the children throughout the school day.

2. **Brain Freeze:** It is important to give our minds a rest—to "freeze" for a short time. The emotional brain takes over when the other brain areas are overworked. Parents and teachers can use a sound to indicate the start of a Brain Freeze. It can be a bell, chime, or light drumming. Teach the child(ren) that once they hear the sound, they should stop whatever they are doing and freeze in a comfortable position. Allow them to lay their head down or curl up on the floor. Encourage them to close their eyes. Try allowing 1 to 3 minutes for Brain Freezes a few times during the child's day at home and at school.

3. **Yoga:** Learn a few simple yoga poses, and practice them with the child at home to prepare the body for the day or to calm down before resting. At school, the teacher can have children lean on the desks and chairs during classroom yoga or simply have them do yoga on the floor.

4. **FADS, JEL, and Compassion Moments:** Take at least one moment of the day to share daily experiences involving emotions and compassion.

chapter 6

Tools,
Schedules,
Posters,
& Activities

Improvement comes through repetition and focus. It is crucial that the four principles (multisensory integration, emotional regulation, executive functioning and mindfulness) be addressed daily. The following chapter provides various resources to make the application of the principles and targets of this program easy for parents and children.

The aim is to provide reproducible resources for the home, classroom, or therapy setting. Feel free to make copies and adapt the resources as you become comfortable with the Self-Regulation and Mindfulness (SAM) program. To start, you will find images of the characters of the Short SAM Stories. Print the images as posters that illustrate the characters during or after the story. Have the child(ren) complete the coloring pages while you talk about the four principles.

EVERYDAY SAM PRACTICES CHART
FOR CLASSROOMS

The following exercises are important to incorporate into daily practice.

	AM (Identify Time/Period)	PM (Identify Time/Period)	Observation Notes
Breath Breaks 3–5 min to blow out the energy (can use feathers, tissues, pinwheels, etc.)			
Brain Freeze Bell, chime, or gentle drum beat can be used to indicate it is time to freeze; turn down lights and have the children stop their activity and get into a comfy position with eyes closed for 1–3 min			
Yoga Pose Take 3–5 min practicing a new yoga pose			
FADS, JEL, and Compassion Moments In place of sharing, use the time to share and discuss moments of FADS, JEL, and compassion experiences from the day or week			
SAM Box Break Take a 3-5 min moment to allow the children time with the items in their SAM Box.			

MILLIE THE ARMADILLO

After coloring, draw some of the items that helped Millie.

MAX THE KANGAROO

What were some things that helped Max?

HARRY THE HIPPOPOTAMUS

What were some things Harry and his classmates learned?

MAKE YOUR SAM BOX

AIM To provide a tool for your child to acknowledge their arousal levels and how they support or impede daily function. Children will determine if their arousal is low (quiet), just right (middle), or high (loud). The SAM Box is useful in a variety of contexts and environments.

YOU WILL NEED

- A small cardboard box, shoebox, or tissue box (a pencil case with zipper can be used instead; instructions to follow)
- Glue
- Brass brad or pushpin
- Construction paper or cardstock (or any other durable material that can be cut into an arrow shape and attached to the box)
- Paint (optional)
- Markers or crayons
- "Feelings" images (provided on page 84)

INSTRUCTIONS

1. Decorate the box by gluing on construction paper or using paint.
2. Draw a circle on the top center of the box to make the "volume guage."
3. Draw an upside-down "Y" to divide the circle into three even sections.
4. Starting at the bottom and going clockwise, color and label the sections: Quiet, Middle, and Loud. Use different colors for each section.
5. Cut an arrow out of construction paper or cardstock.
6. Poke a hole in the center of the circle, and use the brad or pushpin to adhere the arrow to the box.

7. Cut out the Feelings images (on the next page) and place them around the dial, with the "Quiet" image toward the bottom, the "Middle" image at the top left, and the "Loud" image at the top right; you can also draw your own images or use photos of the child.

8. Use the inside of the SAM Box to store preferred sensory items, such as fidgets (see Appendix), a device that plays music, coloring pages, mandalas, exercise cards, tactile bins (bins full of dried rice or beans, marbles, etc.), pinwheels, and bubbles.

9. Be sure to first identify items to support the child when their arousal is loud or quiet. The goal is for them to be in the middle during functional activities.

INSTRUCTIONS IF USING A PENCIL CASE TO MAKE THE SAM BOX

1. Take a small, round piece of cardstock or other durable material and poke a hole in the center.
2. Follow steps 3 through 5 above to make an arrow and volume gage.
3. Take a keychain ring and place through the gage and adhere onto the pencil case.
4. Store sensory items inside the pencil case, as indicated in the previous section.

FEELINGS IMAGES:

_____

Loud

Medium

Quiet

SAM BOX AROUSAL LEVEL CHART

AIM This chart provides a tool to be used in conjunction with a SAM Box for your child to acknowledge their arousal levels and how they support or impede daily function. Children will determine if their arousal is low (Quiet), just right (Middle), or high (Loud). The SAM Box is useful in a variety of contexts and environments.

To start, you will need a blank SAM Box Arousal Level Chart (page 86). Complete it as indicated by the following example.

	Arousal Level	Signs	Change Your Volume: Example
QUIET	Low (provide examples of a low arousal level, such as slow heartbeat and breathing)	Have the child identify their personal signs of a quiet volume; for example, have them look in the mirror and make a "tired" facial expression. Discuss their feelings relating to FADS.	Discuss ways to bring up their arousal; for example, doing wall or chair push-ups, going for a walk, eating something crunchy
MIDDLE	Just right (provide examples of middle arousal, such as medium heartbeat, being alert, paying attention)	Have the child identify their personal signs of a middle volume; for example, have them look in the mirror and make a "calm and alert" facial expression. Discuss the JEL feelings connected to being in the middle.	Discuss ways to keep their arousal in the middle, such as having a water bottle so they can drink water during class.
LOUD	High (provide examples of a high arousal level, such as a racing heartbeat and fast/heavy breathing)	Have the child identify their personal signs of a loud volume. For example, have them look in the mirror and make an "excited" facial expression.	Discuss ways to bring down their arousal; for example, taking deep breaths, sitting on a bean bag chair, eating something chewy

SAM BOX AROUSAL LEVEL CHART

	Arousal Level	Signs	Change Your Volume: Example
QUIET			
MIDDLE			
LOUD			

DAILY SAM SHEET

Child's Name _____   Person Completing Sheet_____

Setting _____   Date _____

AIM To track application of the daily targets for the SAM program. Take a tally of the number of activities for each target that were performed.

TARGET	AM	LUNCH	AFTERNOON	PM (if applicable)	BEDTIME (if applicable)	NOTES
1. Touch and Heavy Work						
2. Hydration and Oral Motor						
3. Metronome and Timing						
4. Right and Left Brain Integration						
5. Patterns and Repetition						
6. Breath and Valsalva						
7. Vision and Sound						
8. Movement						
9. Inhibition						

Signature: _____   Date: _____

WEEKLY SAM SHEET

Child's Name _____   Week of _____

Target (Indicate Totals for Each Day)	Monday	Tuesday	Wednesday	Thursday	Friday	Saturday	Sunday
Touch and Heavy Work							
Hydration and Oral Motor							
Metronome and Timing							
Right and Left Brain Integration							
Patterns and Repetition							
Breath and Valsalva							
Vision and Sound							
Movement							
Inhibition							

Notes:

SAM JOURNAL

AIM To allow children and adults to identify multisensory, emotional regulation, executive functioning, and mindfulness experiences

Before you start you will a journal, or a blank sheet of paper. You may alter the questions to meet the developmental level of the child.

Have the child answer the following questions. Daily or weekly completion may result in better application of the SAM principles.

1. Identify some sensory experiences you had recently. Was there a food you really enjoyed or disliked? What things made you feel relaxed or comfortable? What activities did you experience?

2. What are some examples of you using your "Leader"(the front part of your brain)? Examples: making a good choice, playing nicely with others, listening to adults.

3. Write some examples of when you felt your emotions were out of control. What did you do to quiet them?

4. What are you experiencing right now? How does your body feel? What do you notice around you?

5. Write some examples of when you were compassionate or could have done a better job of being compassionate. How did your actions make other people feel?

EMOTIONAL BINGO

AIM To provide a tool for the child to recognize the JEL and FADS feelings discussed in relation to the four principles.

YOU WILL NEED

- 21 small pieces of paper (index cards or torn pieces of scrap paper)
- Provided BINGO sheet printouts

Using the 21 small pieces of paper, make three sets of each of the seven JEL and FADS feelings (Joy, Enthusiasm, Love, Frustration, Anxiety, Desire, and Sadness), writing each feeling on a separate paper. Place the papers into a container or bag.

Randomly select a paper and note the feeling written on it. Instead of calling out the word, act out the feeling through your facial expressions and body language. Have the child(ren) guess what feeling is being show, then place a mark, coin, or small piece of candy on the corresponding feeling square on the BINGO sheet. Keep going until BINGO is reached with four across, down, or diagonally. You can also use the blank BINGO template to play, writing in the feeling words in a different order.

EMOTIONAL BINGO

JOY	FRUSTRATION	SADNESS	ANXIETY
ANXIETY	ENTHUSIASM	LOVE	DESIRE
FRUSTRATION	ANXIETY	DESIRE	ENTHUSIASM
ENTHUSIASM	LOVE	JOY	SADNESS

EMOTIONAL BINGO

TARGET CARDS

AIM To provide a fun method of implementing the daily targets.

DIRECTIONS Cut out the following cards. On the back of each one, write the name of a preferred activity from the corresponding chapters. Shuffle the cards, and have the child choose an activity every couple of hours during the day. Make copies to add different activities as desired.

TARGET 1	TARGET 2	TARGET 3
TOUCH AND HEAVY WORK	**HYDRATION AND ORAL MOTOR**	**METRONOME AND TIMING**
TARGET 4	TARGET 5	TARGET 6
RIGHT AND LEFT BRAIN INTEGRATION	**PATTERNS AND REPETITION**	**BREATH AND VALSALVA**
TARGET 7	TARGET 8	TARGET 9
VISION AND SOUND	**MOVEMENT**	**INHIBITION**

SAM TACKLE BOX

AIM To provide a convenient, organized method of applying the principles and targets of the SAM program

YOU WILL NEED

- A small tackle box or pillbox
- Select items or laminated pictures of activities and/or sensory items: Items may include images or names of activities, oral motor items such as candy, fidgets (see Appendix) or stress balls, therapy/exercise bands, music, etc.

DIRECTIONS

- Place daily or weekly selected items, activities, or laminated pictures within the container.

- Identify a schedule for the child to retrieve the selected items throughout the day or week.

- You may want to label the outside of the box with images of what is inside, and for added fun, use stickers or other items for the child to decorate their SAM Tackle Box.

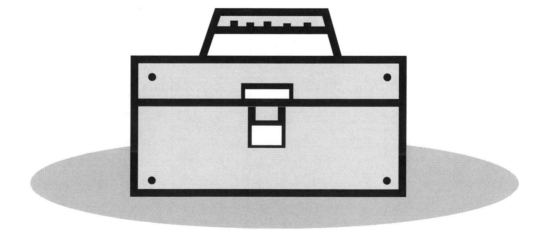

SAM NOOK

AIM To provide an area for children to calm down, decrease sensory stimulation, and prepare for appropriate engagement and interaction

YOU WILL NEED

- A corner sectioned off with a room divider or other objects, a tent, a curtained area, or a table high enough for a child to go under

- Soft seating, such as a bean bag chair, or a ball pit or foam for the child to sit in

- A blanket (preferably weighted) or a sleeping bag for the child to go under

- Other sensory items, such as fidgets (see Appendix), tactile bins (bins full of dried rice or beans, water beads, etc.), essential oil playdough, headphones, weighted objects, a rocking chair, and medicine balls

- Lycra® fabric, which can be secured around a table for an under-the-table hammock swing

- Allow the child to use their SAM Nook during periods of heightened arousal or periodically throughout the day.

SAM PASS

AIM To provide a child the independence and motivation to request what they need to improve their self-regulation

YOU WILL NEED
- The provided image or one of your own
- A lamination machine (or you can print the image on cardboard or other sturdy material)
- A string

DIRECTIONS

1. Laminate and cut out the image, punch a hole in the bottom, and tie a looped string through the hole.

2. Make guidelines for use in your setting.

3. Allow the child to use the SAM Pass to request time in the SAM Nook, to take a walk, to select a sensory activity, or simply to take a time out.

SAM PRESENT

AIM To provide a physical reminder that the present moment is a gift

DIRECTIONS

- Have the child help you select or make a small gift box.

- Utilize the gift box during challenges or periods of upset.

- Remind the child that each day and moment is a gift … that is why it is called "the present." This is especially important for the child to remember during times they are focused on past or possible future events.

- Utilize during a breath break, meditation, or daily target activity if needed.

- Be sure the child has access to their gift. They may start to seek it out as an indicator that the moment may be challenging and a break is needed.

Part Two

chapter 7

The Nine Targets

Now that we have reviewed the foundational principles of the program, let us review the targets. These targets are based on the four principles. Addressing the targets supports the use of the science and evidence previously provided. This chapter gives an overview of the nine daily targets:

1. Touch and heavy work
2. Hydration and oral motor
3. Metronome and timing
4. Right and left brain integration
5. Patterns and repetition
6. Breath and Valsalva
7. Vision and sound
8. Movement
9. Inhibition

TARGET #1: TOUCH AND HEAVY WORK

Touch is the first sense (at the start of life) and last sense (retained at the end of life) we experience. Our skin is our largest organ, so targeting the touch system is powerful. Touch, or tactile input, is a natural part of life. Some children desire touch. They present with seeking behaviors to get their needs met.

Children may seek out input inappropriately, affecting their participation in functional activities. Such behaviors have a connection to the RAS, which is a conduit between the brainstem and the cortex that helps regulate attention. To address inappropriate touch-seeking in children, it is important that they experience touch activities in addition to other sensory stimuli. Presenting desired touch activities along with other sensory activities may enhance the child's ability to process sensory information: A multisensory approach is necessary.

On the other end of the spectrum, some children experience challenges with tactile input. For example, they may become upset or hypervigilant and experience a fight-or-flight reaction when touched. This can occur even when the child is presented with nonthreatening stimuli. Challenges result from the child wearing certain clothing, eating a variety of foods, and interacting with others. As was reviewed in Chapter 1, the RAS plays a vital role in determining to which stimuli we pay attention and how much arousal results. Participating in nonthreatening, purposeful daily touch activities can decrease overreactions. Pairing such activities with a desired stimulus can assist in decreasing the challenges that arise when children are presented with an unwanted stimulus.

Additionally, pain is typically triggered at the areas closest to the surface of the skin. Targeting deep pressure decreases activation of the receptors causing the pain reaction. Prolonged, continuous, and generalized touch also decreases the activation of those receptors, as they respond more quickly to the starting and stopping of stimulation to the skin. The following illustration identifies the levels of touch receptors in the skin.

The free nerve endings and those for sensitive touch are located in the more superficial skin layers than are those for vibration and pressure. When attempting to decrease a child's hyperreaction to light touch, it is crucial to provide deep input by applying pressure to the joints and muscles. Deep pressure input can also occur through physical activity because the receptors for pressure having a connection to the tendons, bones, and muscles. Heavy work is a great method for triggering those receptors.

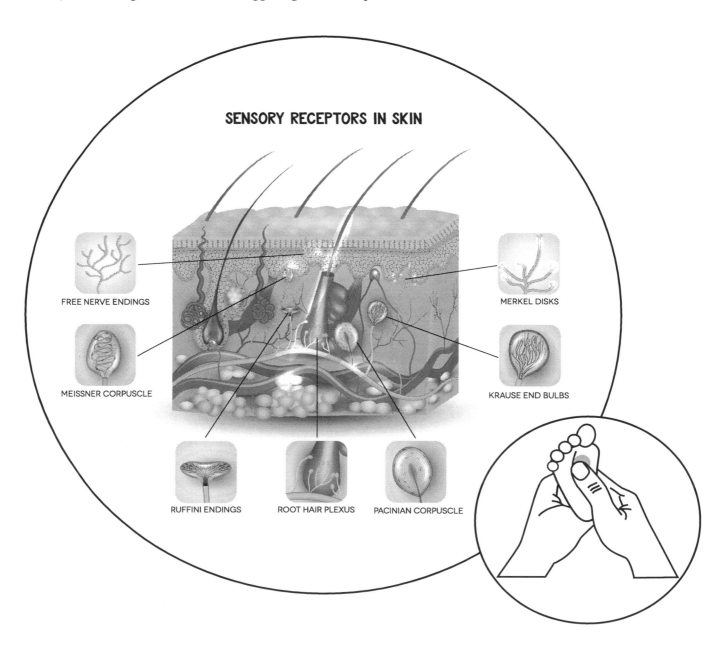

Providing deep pressure input to the body can decrease hyperreactive responses to touch.

Touch can result in the release of calming neurochemicals. This is where heavy work comes into play. Weight bearing, stretching, and pressure can release stress hormones and relax the body. Whether a child has a high or low arousal, heavy work is an approach that may assist them with self-regulation. Stress hormones cause the heart and respiratory rate to increase; they can also enhance hypervigilance and focus and suppression of immunity and digestive systems. Overactivation of stress hormones can lead to decreased activation and use of the front parts of the brain. It is crucial to find ways to release such hormones to enhance executive functioning.

Target #1, Touch and Heavy Work, correlates directly with the principles of multisensory integration and executive functioning. Mindfulness is a component of all of the targets, but for target #1, it plays a special role during touch and heavy work activities requiring focus and repetition. Specific touch and heavy work activities are described in the chapters that follow.

TARGET #2: HYDRATION AND ORAL MOTOR

Hydration of the body is often undervalued. Muscle tension and pain can decrease secondary to proper hydration. If children are dehydrated, they can experience discomfort and hypersensitivity. A strong correlation also exists between hydration and brain function: Drinking proper levels of water can increase focus and attention. Furthermore, the act of swallowing triggers a regulatory response through stimulating nerves connected to the parasympathetic nervous system, which controls rest and digestion.

Oral motor activities involve input to the mouth. There is a strong connection to the brainstem and RAS: When we chew, cranial nerves connected to the parasympathetic nervous system can be calming and organizing. Sucking, eating chewy foods, and rhythmic chewing help to regulate the RAS and produce a calming response. Crunchy foods produce a stimulating reaction in the RAS, enhancing attention and alertness. Children, whether they have high or low arousal levels, may seek out oral motor input. Oral motor input connects to our emotional brain, due to activation of the RAS, and can provide stress relief.

While children may desire input to their mouths for different reasons, attempting to stop the behavior could be unsuccessful and reinforce the undesired behaviors. Target #2, Hydration and Oral Motor, directly correlates with the multisensory integration and emotional regulation principles. There is certainly an indirect correlation with executive function. As with all of the targets, mindfulness is an important aspect.

TARGET #3: METRONOME AND TIMING

Starting and stopping activities helps to activate the front part of the brain as well as the IC. Daily activities enhance attention and focus. Timing and sequencing can help develop organizational skills and improve motor planning. Target #3 introduces the child to fun activities to stimulate their brain. An important component to the activities is the use of a metronome. The brain loves rhythm and repetition. Several bodily functions rely on or produce rhythm. Heartbeat, circadian rhythms, breath rate, and the sucking reflex are just a few of the rhythms of the body.

Interventions based on brain rhythms are an important component of this program and are supported by research. As we participate in various activities and tasks, our brain produces rhythms called brain oscillation. A synchronous rhythm occurs when we participate in focused, repetitive behaviors. For this reason, some children perform self-stimulatory behaviors in a repetitive fashion. While many of these behaviors are discouraged, they actually can produce a good feeling secondary to endorphin release. There are specific methods to enhance such preferred responses in the brain that utilize rhythmic activity. The use of a metronome is one of them. Target #3, Metronome and Timing, relates to the principles of executive functioning and mindfulness.

TARGET #4: RIGHT AND LEFT BRAIN INTEGRATION

The two sides of our brain are not the same. Yes, we generally have the same structures in the left hemisphere as in the right. However, each side of the brain has a somewhat different function. Both sides must work together for successful participation and interaction. Some children have more activity on the left or the right side of the brain. Their behaviors reveal evidence of where the imbalance lies. A child with more left-brain activity may have higher levels of verbal communication and may be analytical, yet can lack social skills and miss the "big picture." Having more activation of the right brain may result in creativity with challenges in more analytical problem-solving abilities.

Luckily, our body activities directly activate our brain. The right side of our body causes activity in the left brain hemisphere and vice versa. Performing activities with both sides of the body can enhance integration of the hemispheres. Target #4, Right and Left Brain Integration, provides activities for this purpose by applying the principle of multisensory integration.

TARGET #5: PATTERNS AND REPETITION

The world functions with rhythm and patterns: the birds flying in the sky, the rotation of the earth, the beautiful patterns made by fireflies. These rhythms keep the world moving. Several body systems produce and require rhythm; for example, our circadian rhythms, heartbeat, breathing, and the suck of a baby feeding. Similarly, our brain and nervous system respond to focus and repetition, which provide a sense of well-being and comfort. Using patterns and repetition is a key component of enhancing self-regulation. Ritualistic behaviors, such as routines, may produce calm feelings. Some rituals support self-regulation, such as practicing meditation. However, ritualistic behaviors often observed as symptoms of ASD (e.g., rocking, spinning) often isolate the child and impede them from interacting with others and the environment. While the child's repetitive actions may not seem to pose much of a threat, there may still be some concerns around safety and development. The more thoughtful use of activities involving patterns and repetition can provide a sense of well-being while enhancing participation and engagement. Target #5, Patterns and Repetition, relates to all of the principles, specifically mindfulness.

TARGET #6: BREATH AND VALSALVA

How do we activate the system for rest and digestion, the parasympathetic nervous system? There are various methods. Deep rhythmic breathing is one of the most powerful methods to activate regulation. The connection between deep breathing and the vagus nerve allows for the heart and breath rates to decrease. There is a release of calming neurochemicals and decrease of stress hormones. However, when we tell children to take a deep breath, they often do the opposite and take shallow, short bursts of air, resulting in the triggering of an excitatory response. It is crucial to utilize methods to assist children in performing correct deep breathing (e.g., have the child lie down and place a stuffed animal on their abdomen and watch the animal rise and fall as they take deep breaths).

Similar to deep breathing, the Valsalva maneuver produces an immediate activation of the parasympathetic nervous system. Parasympathetic nervous system responses, along with other natural reflexes, can improve regulation, attention and focus. For example, both spinning activities and cold temperatures trigger the vagus nerve. Many children spin in attempt to activate the vagus nerve; however, their attempts are usually unsuccessful and result in increased arousal rather than calming. Some children perform self-injurious behavior to elicit calming reactions; a less harmful way for them to get a similar response is to engage in activities involving ice. This is partly due to the fact that the receptors for pain and temperature have the same neurological tracts to the brain. For those challenging children with high thresholds, ice therapy can be a marvelous change agent.

Target #6, Breath and Valsalva, involves techniques to trigger the regulatory responses in our nervous system. Frequent implementation of these activities fine-tunes the function of the IC in teaching our body the feeling of calmness. In addition, children can learn the techniques to implement later during periods of stress and anxiety. Target #6 addresses the principles of emotional regulation and mindfulness.

TARGET #7: VISION AND SOUND

The visual and auditory systems are vital to survival. When dysfunction occurs, severe distress may result. Children who have a sensitivity to light or sound can experience discomfort and physiological stress. Conversely, some children seek out activation in the visual and auditory systems. If these sensations are "highly wired" or organized, a child may utilize them to block out other unwanted stimuli. Appropriately addressing both systems can improve self-regulation.

Activities targeting the visual and auditory systems can decrease hypervigilance and enhance regulation. Such activities must be structured and organized. Inappropriate stimulation or overstimulation can lead to dysregulation. In our brain, there is an area near the RAS that involves both the visual and auditory systems. For example, when you hear an unexpected noise, you turn to look for where it came from. This brain area is hyperresponsive in some children and underresponsive in others. Performing activities that integrate vision and sound can further improve a child's response. Target #7, Vision and Sound directly addresses the principles of multisensory integration and mindfulness. In addition, with the connection to the RAS the other principles are indirectly addressed.

TARGET #8: MOVEMENT

Movement-based activities are very important in the Self-Regulation and Mindfulness program. We previously reviewed how retained primitive reflexes (e.g., Asymmetrical Tonic Neck, Symmetrical Tonic Neck, Moro, Spinal Galant, Palmar, Rooting, Tonic Labyrinthine, Landau) can impair the functioning of some children. In Chapter 4, we identified methods for assessing children in revealing nonintegrated reflexes.

The vestibular system is located within the inner ear. When we move, specifically our head, the receptors are stimulated and send a message through the nervous system to the brain. Fluid in the semicircular canals moves as we rotate our head and move it up and down and from left to right.

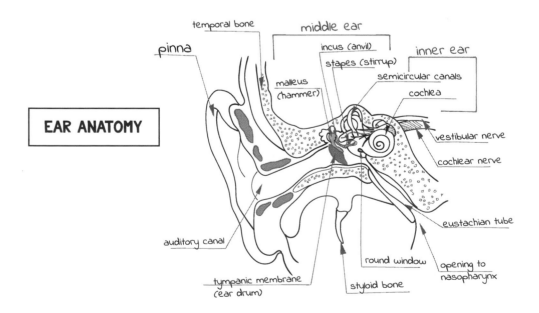

There is a strong connection between movement and vision. As our head moves, our eyes must be able to shift to maintain our gaze. Challenges in disconnecting eye and head movements are correlated with difficulty with activities such as reading, writing, and gross motor skills.

The activities for Target #8 provide opportunities for functional movement and decreasing the activation of the primitive reflexes. Furthermore, children often desire movement and require it throughout their day. Children who are underresponsive and lack physical activity also require enhanced opportunities for movement. Target #8 provides physical movement activities while addressing all of the principles.

TARGET #9: INHIBITION

The ability to stop oneself from making poor decisions develops over time. Some children have significant deficits in this area. Judgment, choice making, and flexibility are possible once nonpreferred behavior is ceased. It is important for children to begin to learn how to stop what they are doing. Many childhood games incorporate starting and stopping, and unspoken playground rules address inhibition of poor behavior. When certain neurodevelopmental conditions arise, theses skills may be hampered. Target #9 provides games and activities to address inhibition. Such activities activate the front part of the brain and the IC. This target addresses all of the principles of this program.

SUMMARY

Having reviewed the nine targets, we now present activities supporting each target. Please be sure to review **Chapter 4** to assist in identifying the child's arousal and threshold levels. You should also reflect on the science behind the program to have an idea of where the child falls on the **Self-Regulation and Mindfulness 7-Level Hierarchy.** The following activities may act as a catalyst to inspire your developing your own plan for meeting the child's needs.

chapter 8

Touch & Heavy Work Activities

The following worksheets are designed to identify the daily target supporting the four principles of multi-sensory integration, emotional regulation, executive functioning and mindfulness. These activities are focused on touch and heavy work, but be sure the child is at the appropriate level for each activity.

At the beginning of each of the following activities, the activity level is identified according to the **Self-Regulation and Mindfulness 7-Level Hierarchy.** As you may recall, Levels 1 through 4 on the hierarchy correspond with higher-level activities, Level 5 corresponds with midlevel activities, and Levels 6 and 7 correspond with foundational-level activities. The Threshold and Arousal Levels Table in Chapter 4 can be used to identify the child's levels. Be sure to keep track of which activities work for the child and their reactions to the activities.

General strategies:

- Massage and personal touch
- Bean bag chairs and cozy corners
- Carrying weighted objects, such as a grocery store basket, library books, or gym equipment, during everyday tasks
- Playing with textures (e.g., during cooking, which is a wonderful opportunity for tactile stimulation)
- Using a multisensory approach (e.g., play background music during an activity or use aromatherapy lotion during a deep pressure massage)

GO FISH

AIM To decrease sensory sensitivity, or high arousal level, through touch

Suggested Starting Hierarchy Level Foundational on page ix

Appropriate Arousal Level High (energetic) or low (lack of response)*

Appropriate Threshold Level High (hyperactive) or (inattentive)*

YOU WILL NEED

- A container, such as a large plastic bin (any size will work, but larger is better)
- Water beads
- Ice cubes to fill the bin (can be performed without ice if needed)
- Gummy fish candy or plastic sea creatures

DIRECTIONS

1. Place water beads and ice into the large container. (You may also freeze the water beads if you feel the child will be safe and not attempt to place them in their mouth.)

2. Hide the gummy fish or plastic sea creatures among the ice cubes.

3. Have the child use their hands to locate the candy or plastic toys.

4. Optional: Talk about how the temperature felt against their skin. Also see if the child can distinguish between two differently shaped items without using their vision.

*The threshold indicates how easily the child detects stimuli, or changes in their environment (low = quick detection; high = slow detection). A child's arousal is the behavioral reaction to stimuli that we can observe.

PINKY TEST

AIM To encourage appropriate exploration with textures

Suggested Starting Hierarchy Level Foundational to midlevel on page ix

Appropriate Arousal Level High (overreaction) or low (lack of response)*

Appropriate Threshold Level Low (hypervigilant) or high (inattentive)*

YOU WILL NEED

- Small jars or sandwich bags
- Items to touch, such as ice cubes, hair gel, cotton balls, dry pasta or rice, dry beans, etc.

DIRECTIONS

1. Place the items in individual jars or sandwich bags.

2. Have the child use their pinky to attempt to touch the various objects.

3. Ask guiding questions to discuss what they feel and their preferences.

4. Provide positive praise for their attempts as well as participation.

5. Encourage the child to use their other fingers, one at a time, to touch the various textures.

*The threshold indicates how easily the child detects stimuli, or changes in their environment
(low = quick detection; high = slow detection). A child's arousal is the behavioral reaction to stimuli that we can observe.

REARRANGE THE ROOM

AIM To perform heavy work to decrease high arousal levels or increase low arousal levels for optimal arousal for functional activities

Suggested Starting Hierarchy Level Foundational on page ix

Appropriate Arousal Level Targets all arousal levels*

Appropriate Threshold Level Targets all thresholds*

YOU WILL NEED

- Furniture

DIRECTIONS

1. Ask the child to help you rearrange the room.

2. This can be for cleaning purposes or actual room set-up.

3. Be sure the items are not too heavy for the child to move.

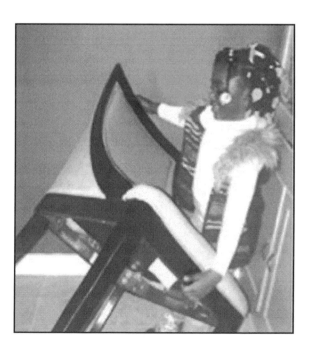

*The threshold indicates how easily the child detects stimuli, or changes in their environment
(low = quick detection; high = slow detection). A child's arousal is the behavioral reaction to stimuli that we can observe.

DRUMMING

AIM To provide pressure and vibration to the joints through a fun and engaging activity

Suggested Starting Hierarchy Level Foundational on page ix

Appropriate Arousal Level Targets all arousal levels*

Appropriate Threshold Level Targets all thresholds*

YOU WILL NEED

- A coffee can or large tin container
- A plastic lid that fits the container or a balloon to be used as the drum head
- A rubber band (if using a balloon)

DIRECTIONS

1. To make a drum out of a coffee can, tightly secure the balloon over the container using the rubber band.

2. Have the child drum along to a recorded song or their own singing, or they can simply have fun drumming as they wish! Remember, enjoy the moment!

*The threshold indicates how easily the child detects stimuli, or changes in their environment
(low = quick detection; high = slow detection). A child's arousal is the behavioral reaction to stimuli that we can observe.

CLAY EMOTIONAL SCULPTURES

AIM To provide a method of self-expression to share feelings and emotions

Suggested Starting Hierarchy Level Midlevel to High on page ix

Appropriate Arousal Level Targets all arousal levels*

Appropriate Threshold Level Targets all thresholds*

YOU WILL NEED

- Playdough or clay

DIRECTIONS

1. Ask the child to share their current feelings and emotions or those they had at a certain time of the day or during a certain experience.

2. Ask them to use the provided materials to make a face or sculpture reflecting the feelings and emotions they experienced in that moment.

*The threshold indicates how easily the child detects stimuli, or changes in their environment (low = quick detection; high = slow detection). A child's arousal is the behavioral reaction to stimuli that we can observe.

CLEAN UP WITH A LAUNDRY BASKET

AIM To provide heavy work to the joints through a fun and engaging activity

Suggested Starting Hierarchy Level Foundational on page ix

Appropriate Arousal Level Targets all arousal levels*

Appropriate Threshold Level Targets all thresholds*

YOU WILL NEED

- A laundry basket or other container with handles

DIRECTIONS

1. Have the child use the basket to clean up items around the room.

2. Be sure they are carrying the basket around the room.

3. Make it more fun by using a timer or having the child race a friend.

*The threshold indicates how easily the child detects stimuli, or changes in their environment
(low = quick detection; high = slow detection). A child's arousal is the behavioral reaction to stimuli that we can observe.

WARM AND COZY

AIM To provide tactile input to the body to decrease arousal and enhance comfort

Suggested Starting Hierarchy Level Foundational on page ix

Appropriate Arousal Level High (overreaction or hyperactive)*

Appropriate Threshold Level Low (hypervigilant) or high (energetic)*

YOU WILL NEED

- Clothing or towels recently removed from the dryer (or recently ironed)

DIRECTIONS

1. Place the clothing or towel on the child following bath time or when changing clothing.

2. Perform friction rubs by quickly moving the towel or your hands over the clothing for added input.

3. The warmth may decrease high arousal to prepare the child for the day or for rest.

*The threshold indicates how easily the child detects stimuli, or changes in their environment
(low = quick detection; high = slow detection). A child's arousal is the behavioral reaction to stimuli that we can observe.

DEEP PRESSURE INPUT

AIM To provide deep pressure proprioceptive input to the body to decrease arousal and enhance comfort

Suggested Starting Hierarchy Level Foundational on page ix

Appropriate Arousal Level High (overreaction or hyperactive)*

Appropriate Threshold Level Low (hypervigilant) or high (energetic)*

YOU WILL NEED

- Nothing if you are performing muscle and joint compression
- A ball pit or bean bag chair if using other stimuli

DIRECTIONS

1. Before performing joint and muscle compressions, be sure to consult a trained professional, such as an occupational therapist. Provide pressure to the muscle bellies of the arms, legs, and back.

2. Joint compressions can be performed on the limbs.

3. You may also have the child sit in a ball pit or on a bean bag chair while you provide gentle pressure over their body.

*The threshold indicates how easily the child detects stimuli, or changes in their environment (low = quick detection; high = slow detection). A child's arousal is the behavioral reaction to stimuli that we can observe.

ANIMAL WALKS

AIM To perform muscle and joint input to the body to decrease arousal or enhance attentiveness

Suggested Starting Hierarchy Level Foundational on page ix

Appropriate Arousal Level High (overreaction) or low (lack of response)*

Appropriate Threshold Level Low (hypervigilant) or high (inattentive)*

YOU WILL NEED

- An open area in which to move around

DIRECTIONS

1. Have the child perform bear walks and crab walks across the floor.

2. Use a timer or have the child race a friend to make it more fun.

3. View the images below for guidance.

Bear Walk

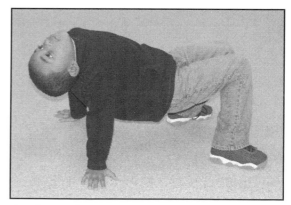

Crab Walk

*The threshold indicates how easily the child detects stimuli, or changes in their environment
(low = quick detection; high = slow detection). A child's arousal is the behavioral reaction to stimuli that we can observe.

Chapter 9

Hydration &
Oral Motor Activities

This chapter uses activities of hydration and oral motor input to help identify the second daily target.

At the beginning of each of the following activities, the activity level is identified according to the **Self-Regulation and Mindfulness 7-Level Hierarchy.** As you may recall, Levels 1 through 4 on the hierarchy correspond with higher-level activities, Level 5 corresponds with midlevel activities, and Levels 6 and 7 correspond with foundational-level activities. The Threshold and Arousal Levels Table in Chapter 4 can be used to identify the child's level. Be sure to keep track of which activities work for the child and their reactions to the activities.

- Use straws. Fun, silly straws can engage the child.
- If the child is reluctant to try new food items, come up with a playful activity that allows them to touch a food before eating it.
- Remember to use a multisensory approach. Use music, comforting smells, or touch during these activities.

STRAW EXPLORATION

AIM To decrease sensory-seeking behaviors and provide an organizing activity to enhance appropriate attention levels

Suggested Starting Hierarchy Level Foundational on page ix

Appropriate Arousal Level All arousal levels*

Appropriate Threshold Level All thresholds*

YOU WILL NEED

- Long straws in addition to a few straws cut in half

- Thick substances, such as yogurt, smoothies, or ice cream (preferably cold substances for children with high thresholds)

DIRECTIONS

1. Explore the use of both the long and short straws with the various substances.

2. If the child is unable to suck with a long straw, have them try a short one.
   Optional: Try having the child use the straw to transfer ice chips from one cup to another through sucking with the straw then releasing.

3. If the child has difficulty sucking, you can place your finger over the top of the straw to suspend the liquid in the straw, then place it in the child's mouth.

4. For added fun, have the child help you with yogurt and smoothie recipes.

*The threshold indicates how easily the child detects stimuli, or changes in their environment
(low = quick detection; high = slow detection). A child's arousal is the behavioral reaction to stimuli that we can observe.

STICKY CHEEKS

AIM To provide an organizing activity to enhance appropriate attention levels and enhance input to the mouth and tongue

Suggested Starting Hierarchy Level Foundational on page ix

Appropriate Arousal Level High (energetic) or low (lack of response)*

Appropriate Threshold Level High (hyperactive) or (inattentive)*

YOU WILL NEED

- Sticky food (e.g., peanut or fruit butters, fruit leather)

- Eating utensil

DIRECTIONS

1. Place a small amount of the food item on the inside of the child's cheeks and/or roof of the mouth.

2. Have the child use their tongue to retrieve the food.

*The threshold indicates how easily the child detects stimuli, or changes in their environment (low = quick detection; high = slow detection) A child's arousal is the behavioral reaction to stimuli that we can observe.

WATER BOTTLE

AIM To provide an organizing activity to enhance appropriate attention levels and enhance input to the mouth and tongue

Suggested Starting Hierarchy Level Foundational on page ix

Appropriate Arousal Level All arousal levels*

Appropriate Threshold Level All thresholds*

YOU WILL NEED

- A water bottle with a spout or a hole poked in the top

DIRECTIONS

1. This one is very simple. Have the child drink the water.

2. The use of a spout or hole in the top of the bottle is to promote resistive sucking to further enhance attention to and organization of the sensory system.

3. Take advantage of the moment for a mindful discussion about the child's feelings and arousal level.

*The threshold indicates how easily the child detects stimuli, or changes in their environment (low = quick detection; high = slow detection). A child's arousal is the behavioral reaction to stimuli that we can observe.

CRUNCHY OR CHEWY?

AIM To provide an organizing activity to enhance appropriate attention levels and enhance input to the mouth and tongue

Suggested Starting Hierarchy Level Foundational on page ix

Appropriate Arousal Level All arousal levels*

Appropriate Threshold Level All thresholds*

YOU WILL NEED

- A variety of snacks, both crunchy and chewy

DIRECTIONS

1. Have the child explore the various food textures.

2. Discuss how a food feels in the child's mouth and/or observe their reactions.

3. Typically, crunchy foods are alerting and chewy foods are calming.

4. Identify the child's needs based on their arousal level.

5. Based on your observations, choose appropriate foods to have readily available throughout the child's day for oral motor input. Place them in the child's SAM Box if appropriate.

*The threshold indicates how easily the child detects stimuli, or changes in their environment
(low = quick detection; high = slow detection). A child's arousal is the behavioral reaction to stimuli that we can observe.

ICE POPS

AIM To provide an organizing activity to enhance appropriate attention levels and enhance input to the mouth and tongue

Suggested Starting Hierarchy Level Foundational on page ix

Appropriate Arousal Level All arousal levels*

Appropriate Threshold Level All thresholds*

YOU WILL NEED

- Ice pop molds, an ice tray, or paper cups
- Ice pop sticks (optional: lollipop sticks)
- Fruit and fruit juice

DIRECTIONS

1. Take the molds, ice tray, or paper cups and place fruit and fruit juice in them.

2. Place a lollipop or ice pop stick in the center of each mold, ice tray section, or cup. Use a piece of fruit to hold it in place.

3. Put the molds, ice tray, or paper cups in the freezer.

4. Once the ice pops have frozen, enjoy! It is best to have the child eat before an organized activity, play date, or doctor's visit. (Be sure to use caution when giving small ice pops to children, as they can be a choking hazard.)

*The threshold indicates how easily the child detects stimuli, or changes in their environment (low = quick detection; high = slow detection). A child's arousal is the behavioral reaction to stimuli that we can observe.

chapter 10

Metronome, Timing, & Sequencing Activities

This chapter is focused on the metronome, timing and sequencing activities. They will help you to identify the third daily target and enhance focus, attention, and coordination in children.

At the beginning of each of the following activities, the activity level is identified according to the **Self-Regulation and Mindfulness 7-Level Hierarchy.** As you may recall, Levels 1 through 4 on the hierarchy correspond with higher-level activities, Level 5 corresponds with midlevel activities, and Levels 6 and 7 correspond with foundational-level activities. The Threshold and Arousal Levels Table in Chapter 4 can be used to identify the child's levels. Be sure to keep track of which activities work for the child and their reactions to the activities.

SWINGING

AIM To decrease sensory avoiding and inattentive behaviors and provide an organizing activity to enhance appropriate attention levels

Suggested Starting Hierarchy Level Foundational on page ix

Appropriate Arousal Level High (overreaction) or low (lack of response)*

Appropriate Threshold Level High (hypervigilant) or (inattentive)*

YOU WILL NEED

- A swing (indoors or outdoors), hammock, or stretchy fabric/bedding sheet for small children
- A metronome, metronome app or music

DIRECTIONS

1. Use a metronome, metronome app, or rhythmic music as a beat to which to swing the child.

2. Be sure to swing within the chosen rhythm and only in a straight line.

3. For children with anxiety or fearful reactions, choose slow, predictable rhythms.

4. For children who are inattentive, you can use faster, less predictable rhythms.

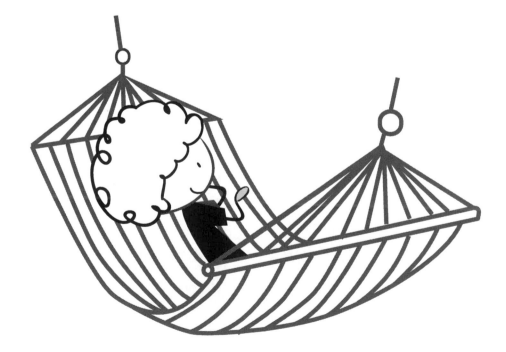

*The threshold indicates how easily the child detects stimuli, or changes in their environment (low = quick detection; high = slow detection). A child's arousal is the behavioral reaction to stimuli that we can observe.

METRONOME WRITING

AIM To decrease hyperactivity and inattentive behaviors and provide an organizing activity to enhance functional participation

Suggested Starting Hierarchy Level Midlevel to high on page ix

Appropriate Arousal Level High (energetic) or low (lack of response)*

Appropriate Threshold Level High (hyperactive) or (inattentive)*

YOU WILL NEED

- A metronome, metronome app or music
- Paper
- A writing utensil

DIRECTIONS

1. Use fast rhythms for children who are typically inattentive and have low arousal.

2. For children with high energy levels, use slow rhythms.

3. Perform a writing activity with the metronome or music in the background.

4. Over time, watch as the child's brain waves start to get in tune with the rhythm.

5. You can use the same method with reading and math activities.

*The threshold indicates how easily the child detects stimuli, or changes in their environment (low = quick detection; high = slow detection). A child's arousal is the behavioral reaction to stimuli that we can observe.

METRONOME EXERCISES

AIM To decrease hyperactivity and inattentive behaviors and provide an organizing activity to enhance functional participation

Suggested Starting Hierarchy Level Midlevel to high on page ix

Appropriate Arousal Level All arousal levels*

Appropriate Threshold Level All threshold levels*

YOU WILL NEED

- A metronome or metronome app

DIRECTIONS

1. Use slow rhythms for children with high arousal levels and fast rhythms for children with low arousal levels.

2. Have the child perform various activities, such as push-ups, crossing the midline, jumping jacks, ladder walks, and animal walks to the beat of the metronome.

*The threshold indicates how easily the child detects stimuli, or changes in their environment (low = quick detection; high = slow detection). A child's arousal is the behavioral reaction to stimuli that we can observe.

chapter 11

Right & Left Brain Integration Activities

This chapter is designed with activities to assist in integrating the right and left brain through identifying the fourth daily target that supports the four principles of multisensory integration, emotional regulation, executive functioning and mindfulness.

At the beginning of each of the following activities, the activity level is identified according to the **Self-Regulation and Mindfulness 7-Level Hierarchy.** As you may recall, Levels 1 through 4 on the hierarchy correspond with higher-level activities, Level 5 corresponds with midlevel activities, and Levels 6 and 7 correspond with foundational-level activities. The Threshold and Arousal Levels Table in Chapter 4 can be used to identify the child's level. Be sure to keep track of which activities work for the child and their reactions to the activities.

XYZ

AIM To enhance attention and provide an organizing activity to prepare the brain and body for work

Suggested Starting Hierarchy Level Midlevel to high on page ix

Appropriate Arousal Level All arousal levels*

Appropriate Threshold Level All thresholds*

YOU WILL NEED

- A metronome or metronome app

DIRECTIONS

1. Model the three poses (images on the next page). Bring your arms down between each pose and each repetition, with the exception of Pose Z (for which you move the arms in and out, as shown in the images).

2. Once the child understands the moves, instruct them to follow you, or have them perform the pose a certain number of times on their own (e.g., four of each, then two of each, then one of each).

3. Remind the child to bring the arms down between Poses X and Y.

4. You can print out pictures of the moves if the child needs more guidance.

5. Use the metronome so the child can perform the activity to a steady rhythm.

*The threshold indicates how easily the child detects stimuli, or changes in their environment (low = quick detection; high = slow detection). A child's arousal is the behavioral reaction to stimuli that we can observe.

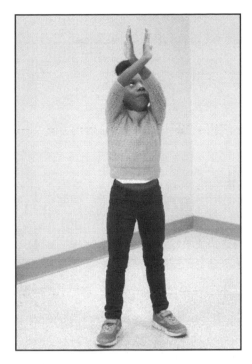

Pose X: Cross the arms in front

Pose Y: Raise the arms up and out

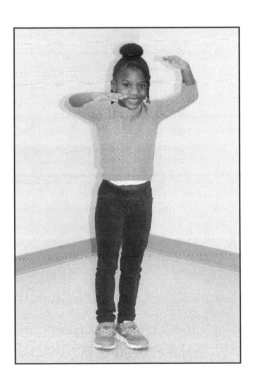

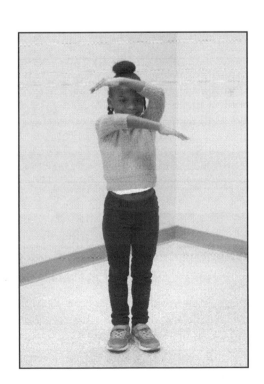

Pose Z: Move the arms in and out

WRITING WITH THE OPPOSITE HAND

AIM To enhance attention and provide an organizing activity to prepare the brain and body for work

Suggested Starting Hierarchy Level Midlevel to high on page ix

Appropriate Arousal Level All arousal levels*

Appropriate Threshold Level All thresholds*

YOU WILL NEED

- A metronome or metronome app (optional)
- A writing utensil
- Paper

DIRECTIONS

1. Have the child perform a writing activity with their nondominant (opposite) hand, with and without the metronome.

2. You can choose to have the child draw or color instead of write, depending on their developmental level.

3. Have the child try performing other tabletop tasks with the opposite hand. For a challenge, have them try to tie their shoes!

*The threshold indicates how easily the child detects stimuli, or changes in their environment (low = quick detection; high = slow detection). A child's arousal is the behavioral reaction to stimuli that we can observe.

BILATERAL EXERCISES

AIM To enhance attention and provide an organizing activity to prepare the brain and body for work

Suggested Starting Hierarchy Level Midlevel to high on page ix

Appropriate Arousal Level All arousal levels*

Appropriate Threshold Level All thresholds*

YOU WILL NEED

- An open area, playground or a rock climbing wall

DIRECTIONS

1. Have the child perform various exercises incorporating both sides of the body and crossing the midline.

2. Review the images to follow as examples.

 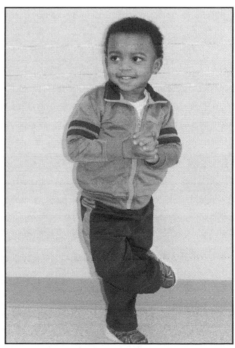

*The threshold indicates how easily the child detects stimuli, or changes in their environment (low = quick detection; high = slow detection). A child's arousal is the behavioral reaction to stimuli that we can observe.

chapter 12

Patterns & Repetition Activities

This chapter uses activities to identify the fifth daily target and to integrate patterns and repetition in an effective way.

At the beginning of each of the following activities, the activity level is identified according to the **Self-Regulation and Mindfulness 7-Level Hierarchy.** As you may recall, Levels 1 through 4 on the hierarchy correspond with higher-level activities, Level 5 corresponds with midlevel activities, and Levels 6 and 7 correspond with foundational-level activities. The Threshold and Arousal Levels Table in Chapter 4 can be used to identify the child's levels. Be sure to keep track of which activities work for the child and their reactions to the activities.

MINDFUL MEDITATION

AIM To enhance attention and mindful awareness of the senses and others around

Suggested Starting Hierarchy Level Foundational on page ix

Appropriate Arousal Level All arousal levels*

Appropriate Threshold Level All thresholds*

YOU WILL NEED

- Items for the child to hold, such as rocks, ice cubes, flowers, a snow globe, walnuts
- A quiet environment
- A chime (optional)

DIRECTIONS

1. Have the child hold the selected item and view all of its characteristics.

2. Ask them to share what they see.

3. Use a chime to start and stop the session.

*The threshold indicates how easily the child detects stimuli, or changes in their environment
(low = quick detection; high = slow detection). A child's arousal is the behavioral reaction to stimuli that we can observe.

MAZES

AIM To enhance attention and mindful awareness and prepare the mind to work

Suggested Starting Hierarchy Level Midlevel to high on page ix

Appropriate Arousal Level All arousal levels*

Appropriate Threshold Level All thresholds*

YOU WILL NEED

- Mazes, such as the one below (be sure to select mazes that are age appropriate for the child)

DIRECTIONS

1. Encourage the child to complete the maze.

2. Provide help as needed.

3. Be sure to discuss their feelings and provide praise when appropriate.

*The threshold indicates how easily the child detects stimuli, or changes in their environment
(low = quick detection; high = slow detection). A child's arousal is the behavioral reaction to stimuli that we can observe.

RHYTHMIC CLEANING

AIM To enhance attention and mindful awareness of the moment

Suggested Starting Hierarchy Level Midlevel to high on page ix

Appropriate Arousal Level All arousal levels*

Appropriate Threshold Level All thresholds*

YOU WILL NEED

- Cleaning tools, such as a broom, mop, or vacuum

DIRECTIONS

1. Come up with a song for the child to sing while cleaning, or play a metronome or music.

2. Encourage the child to use a pattern, such as sweeping to the rhythm.

3. Discuss how they feel before and after the activity, and don't forget to thank them for their help!

*The threshold indicates how easily the child detects stimuli, or changes in their environment
(low = quick detection; high = slow detection). A child's arousal is the behavioral reaction to stimuli that we can observe.

MANDALAS

AIM To enhance attention and mindful awareness of the senses and others around

Suggested Starting Hierarchy Level Midlevel to high on page ix

Appropriate Arousal Level All arousal levels*

Appropriate Threshold Level All thresholds*

YOU WILL NEED

- A printout of a mandala, such as the image that follows
- Crayons, colored pencils, paint, or blow pens
- Playdough (optional)

DIRECTIONS

1. Have the child decorate the mandala on page 138 as they desire.

2. You can have them color or blow paint on it with a straw or blow pen.

3. For younger children, have them use playdough to create a circular pattern.

*The threshold indicates how easily the child detects stimuli, or changes in their environment
(low = quick detection; high = slow detection). A child's arousal is the behavioral reaction to stimuli that we can observe.

138

SMELL DOUGH

AIM To enhance attention and mindful awareness of the senses and others around

Suggested Starting Hierarchy Level Foundational on page ix

Appropriate Arousal Level All arousal levels*

Appropriate Threshold Level All thresholds*

YOU WILL NEED

- Playdough
- Essential oils

DIRECTIONS

1. Mix drops of essential oils into playdough.

2. Use lavender and wood smells for calming.

3. Use citrus smells to increase arousal.

*The threshold indicates how easily the child detects stimuli, or changes in their environment (low = quick detection; high = slow detection). A child's arousal is the behavioral reaction to stimuli that we can observe.

MAPPING EMOTIONS

AIM To enhance attention and mindful awareness of feelings and emotions

Suggested Starting Hierarchy Level Midlevel to high on page ix

Appropriate Arousal Level All arousal levels*

Appropriate Threshold Level All thresholds*

YOU WILL NEED

- A printout of a body (located on next page)
- A writing utensil

DIRECTIONS

1. Have the child color on the body image where their emotions are felt in the present moment.

2. You can use various copies of the image to represent how they felt during certain scenarios, and then discuss them with the child.

3. Be sure to discuss ways to calm down or support their feelings.

*The threshold indicates how easily the child detects stimuli, or changes in their environment
(low = quick detection; high = slow detection). A child's arousal is the behavioral reaction to stimuli that we can observe.

LABYRINTH

AIM To enhance attention and organize the mind and body

Suggested Starting Hierarchy Level Foundational on page ix

Appropriate Arousal Level All arousal levels*

Appropriate Threshold Level All thresholds*

YOU WILL NEED

- Any of the following items to make a large labyrinth pattern on the floor or a smaller one on a tabletop:
  - Chalk
  - Rocks
  - Leaves
  - Tape
  - Sand
  - Sticks
- A cardboard box divided into a labyrinth with popsicle sticks or tape
- A labyrinth image projected on the floor
- A labyrinth app or computer game

DIRECTIONS

1. Encourage the child to complete the labyrinth as indicated.

2. They may walk through it if it is a large labyrinth created on the floor, use their finger if the labyrinth is smaller (i.e., a divided cardboard box, a tabletop labyrinth), or play an electronic labyrinth game.

3. You may have them follow you if needed.

4. Be sure to encourage them to not get frustrated; help them see it as a challenge.

*The threshold indicates how easily the child detects stimuli, or changes in their environment
(low = quick detection; high = slow detection). A child's arousal is the behavioral reaction to stimuli that we can observe.

chapter 13

Breathing & Valsalva Activities

This chapter focuses on identifying the sixth daily target. Utilizing activities to activate a regulatory response with breathing techniques and the valsalva maneuver.

At the beginning of each of the following activities, the activity level is identified according to the **Self-Regulation and Mindfulness 7-Level Hierarchy.** As you may recall, Levels 1 through 4 on the hierarchy correspond with higher-level activities, Level 5 corresponds with midlevel activities, and Levels 6 and 7 correspond with foundational-level activities. The Threshold and Arousal Levels Table in Chapter 4 can be used to identify the child's levels. Be sure to keep track of which activities work for the child and their reactions to the activities.

General strategies:

- Focus on the exhalation and blowing.
- Heavy work also triggers a Valsalva response to activate the vagus nerve.
- Humming, chanting, and singing are other great activities.
- Incorporate a multisensory approach by engaging the child to reflect on their internal sensations and stimuli around them.

HOMEMADE KAZOO

AIM To enhance attention and provide an organizing activity to prepare the brain and body for work

Suggested Starting Hierarchy Level Midlevel to high on page ix

Appropriate Arousal Level All arousal levels*

Appropriate Threshold Level All thresholds*

YOU WILL NEED

- A cardboard tube
- Wax paper
- A rubber band

DIRECTIONS

1. Punch holes along the top of the cardboard tube.

2. Cut a small square of wax paper to cover the tube's bottom opening.

3. Secure the square in place using the rubber band.

4. Instruct the child to hum or blow deeply into the kazoo to make sounds.

*The threshold indicates how easily the child detects stimuli, or changes in their environment
(low = quick detection; high = slow detection). A child's arousal is the behavioral reaction to stimuli that we can observe.

ICE THERAPY

AIM To enhance attention and provide an organizing activity to prepare the brain and body for work

Suggested Starting Hierarchy Level Foundational on page ix

Appropriate Arousal Level High (energetic) or low (lack of response)*

Appropriate Threshold Level High (hyperactive) or (inattentive)*

YOU WILL NEED

- An ice tray
- Finger paints
- Small figures, beads, or jewels frozen inside of ice cubes
- A frozen water bottle or a paper cup full of frozen water

DIRECTIONS

1. There are a variety of options for ice therapy:
    a. You can freeze the finger paint and have the child use it to make artwork. (It still can be used as paint when frozen!).
    b. You can freeze small items inside of ice cubes and have the child hold them to melt the ice and retrieve the item inside.
    c. You can use a frozen water bottle or paper cup full of frozen water to provide a deep pressure massage.

2. Be creative! Children with a high threshold respond well to ice therapy!

*The threshold indicates how easily the child detects stimuli, or changes in their environment (low = quick detection; high = slow detection). A child's arousal is the behavioral reaction to stimuli that we can observe.

BREATHING WITH A TOY

AIM To enhance attention and provide an organizing activity to prepare the brain and body for work

Suggested Starting Hierarchy Level Midlevel to high on page ix

Appropriate Arousal Level All arousal levels*

Appropriate Threshold Level All thresholds*

YOU WILL NEED

- A stuffed animal or other lightweight toy
- A quiet space
- Floor or table space on which the child can lie down

DIRECTIONS

1. Have the child lie on their back.

2. Place the selected item on their belly.

3. Count as they inhale and exhale and watch the item rise and fall with the child's breathing.

4. Challenge them to make the toy fall very slowly by increasing the count during their exhalation.

5. See what number they can reach while counting.

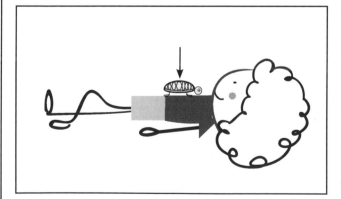 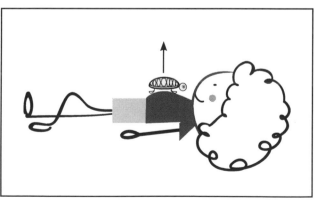

*The threshold indicates how easily the child detects stimuli, or changes in their environment (low = quick detection; high = slow detection). A child's arousal is the behavioral reaction to stimuli that we can observe.

THE TRUMPET

AIM To enhance attention and provide an organizing activity to prepare the brain and body for work or to help the child calm down during times of high arousal or distress

Suggested Starting Hierarchy Level Midlevel to high on page ix

Appropriate Arousal Level All arousal levels*

Appropriate Threshold Level All thresholds*

YOU WILL NEED

- A quiet space

DIRECTIONS

1. As in the image that follows, ask the child to place their thumb tip in their mouth.

2. Have them fill their cheeks with air, not allowing any to escape.

3. Count for 3 to 5 seconds, then repeat.

4. Discuss how they felt before, during, and after the activity.

5. Remind them to use their "trumpet" if they feel upset or have a lot of energy to let out.

*The threshold indicates how easily the child detects stimuli, or changes in their environment
(low = quick detection; high = slow detection). A child's arousal is the behavioral reaction to stimuli that we can observe.

SLOW BREATHING

AIM To enhance attention and provide an organizing activity to prepare the brain and body for work or to help the child calm down during times of high arousal or distress

Suggested Starting Hierarchy Level Foundational on page ix

Appropriate Arousal Level All arousal levels*

Appropriate Threshold Level All thresholds*

YOU WILL NEED

- Any of the following materials, as various activities may be used
  - Straws and feathers
  - Plastic or paper cups and ping pong balls
  - Cheese cloth, a water bottle, a rubber band, and bubbles
  - Putty or slime

DIRECTIONS

1. Remember that the intention is to increase exhalation time.

2. Have the child use the straws to blow feathers across the floor or another surface. They can also blow feathers in the air with you to see who can keep them up the longest.

3. Blowing bubbles is great for all ages. Share with the child that the bubbles are "breath balls." The more they produce, the better.

4. Cut an opening in the front of paper cups the size of a ping pong ball to create "doors." Have the child use a straw to blow a ping pong ball across the floor to the cups. Have children race to see who can get their ball into a cup first.

5. Blow a bubble snake using a water bottle, cheesecloth, rubber band, and bubbles: Cut off the bottom of the bottle and cover with cheesecloth. Secure with the rubber band. Dip the bottle into bubbles. Have the child blow through the top to create bubbles.

6. Have the child blow bubbles into putty or slime using a straw.

*The threshold indicates how easily the child detects stimuli, or changes in their environment (low = quick detection; high = slow detection). A child's arousal is the behavioral reaction to stimuli that we can observe.

chapter 14

Vision & Sound Activities

This chapter will help identify the seventh daily target using activities involving vision and sound to activate a regulatory response and exercise those systems.

At the beginning of each of the following activities, the activity level is identified according to the **Self-Regulation and Mindfulness 7-Level Hierarchy.** As you may recall, Levels 1 through 4 on the hierarchy correspond with higher-level activities, Level 5 corresponds with midlevel activities, and Levels 6 and 7 correspond with foundational-level activities. The Threshold and Arousal Levels Table in Chapter 4 can be used to identify the child's levels. Be sure to keep track of which activities work for the child and their reactions to the activities.

General strategies:

- Use flashlights for scanning activities. Turn down the lights for flashlight tag.
- "I spy" and "hidden picture" games are great visual activities.
- "Follow the leader" and "I'm thinking of an animal, what could it be" games stimulate the auditory system.
- Use music and visual stimuli together to optimize the multisensory approach.

EYE YOGA

AIM To enhance attention and provide an organizing activity to prepare the brain and body for work

Suggested Starting Hierarchy Level Midlevel to high on page ix

Appropriate Arousal Level All arousal levels*

Appropriate Threshold Level All thresholds*

YOU WILL NEED

- A quiet space

DIRECTIONS

1. Ask the child to close their eyes while gently inhaling.

2. Have them try moving their eyes with their eyes closed (e.g., looking up and down).

3. With the eyes open, have the child extend their arm in front of them at eye level with their thumb raised.

4. Have them use their thumb to visually track while keeping their head static.

5. Instruct the child to move their thumb toward their nose and away.

6. Have them move their arm slowly away from the center of their body and then toward the side while following their thumb with their eyes.

7. Remind them not to move their head.

8. Have the child repeat for three or four times, remembering to breathe.

9. You may use chimes or music in the background.

*The threshold indicates how easily the child detects stimuli, or changes in their environment (low = quick detection; high = slow detection). A child's arousal is the behavioral reaction to stimuli that we can observe.

AUDITORY GUESS WHO

AIM To enhance attention and provide exercise to the auditory system

Suggested Starting Hierarchy Level Midlevel to high on page ix

Appropriate Arousal Level High (energetic) or low (lack of response)*

Appropriate Threshold Level High (hyperactive or inattentive)*

YOU WILL NEED

- A quiet space
- A smartphone, computer, or mp3 player

DIRECTIONS

1. Select various sounds, such as animal noises, babies crying or babbling, and other sounds typically found in the child's environment.

2. Have them guess what they are hearing.

3. If more than one child is participating, see who can identify the most sounds.

*The threshold indicates how easily the child detects stimuli, or changes in their environment (low = quick detection; high = slow detection). A child's arousal is the behavioral reaction to stimuli that we can observe.

LAVA BOTTLE

AIM To decrease hyperactivity and inattentive behaviors and provide an organizing activity to enhance functional participation

Suggested Starting Hierarchy Level Midlevel to high on page ix

Appropriate Arousal Level High (energetic or overreacting)*

Appropriate Threshold Level High (hyperactive) or low (hypervigilant)*

YOU WILL NEED

- Cooking oil
- Food coloring
- A water bottle full of water
- A funnel
- An antacid or other fizzing tablet

DIRECTIONS

1. Pour a tablespoon of oil into the water.

2. Drop in a few drops of food coloring.

3. Place the fizz tablet in the bottle.

4. Have the child watch the bubbles move up and down.

5. You can also use lava lamps or Snoezelen rooms for a similar experience.

*The threshold indicates how easily the child detects stimuli, or changes in their environment
(low = quick detection; high = slow detection). A child's arousal is the behavioral reaction to stimuli that we can observe.

I SPY BOTTLE

AIM To decrease hyperactivity and inattentive behaviors and provide an organizing activity to exercise the visual system

Suggested Starting Hierarchy Level Midlevel to high on page ix

Appropriate Arousal Level High (energetic or overreacting)*

Appropriate Threshold Level High (hyperactive) or low (hypervigilant)*

YOU WILL NEED

- A glass or plastic bottle
- Small beads, coins, jewels, or other items
- Dry rice, beans, or pasta

DIRECTIONS

1. Use a funnel if needed to place a small amount of the selected dry rice, beans, or pasta in the bottle.

2. Alternate adding in some of small beads, coins, jewels, or other items and more layers of your base substance.

3. Have the child view the bottle to see how many items they spy, one of the beads, coins, or jewels.

*The threshold indicates how easily the child detects stimuli, or changes in their environment
(low = quick detection; high = slow detection). A child's arousal is the behavioral reaction to stimuli that we can observe.

HEADPHONES

AIM To decrease hyperactivity and hypervigilant behaviors and enhance attention

Suggested Starting Hierarchy Level Foundational on page ix

Appropriate Arousal Level All arousal levels*

Appropriate Threshold Level All thresholds*

YOU WILL NEED

- Regular or noise-cancelling headphones
- Music (optional)

DIRECTIONS

1. Have the child listen to music with headphones.

   a. Children who are inattentive may respond to upbeat, unpredictable music.

   b. Children who are anxious require rhythmic, predictable music.

   c. Children who are sensitive to sound may benefit from wearing noise-cancelling headphones rather than listening to music.

chapter 15

Movement Activities

This chapter includes activities that involve movement and decrease primitive reflex activities and identifies the eighth daily target.

Note: All children need movement. The following activities encourage organized and structured exercise. The format is slightly different than that in the preceding chapters. The poses described are necessary for children suspected of having retained primitive reflexes.

General strategies:

- Allow for movement breaks, making sure that the activities are organized and involve weight bearing, such as yoga, Pilates, or the activities outlined in this chapter.
- Use ankle or wrist weights to enhance input for children with high thresholds. (The weights should be no more than 10% of the child's body weight to start.)
- Incorporate music or a metronome in the background or try using blindfolds to enhance the multisensory experience.

BALL PLAY

AIM To enhance movement for younger children or those with developmental delays in gross motor ability

YOU WILL NEED

- A large therapy or yoga ball
- Space to move around
- A mat (optional)

DIRECTIONS

1. Use play to encourage the child to explore different positions on the ball.

2. Have the child roll on the ball while supporting their trunk or extremities.

3. Have the child engage their core by sitting on the ball and doing sit-ups while holding their thigh area. (You may use your legs to hold to ball for support.)

WALL PUSH-UPS AND SITS

AIM To allow the opportunity for movement to increase attention and prepare for work

YOU WILL NEED

- An open wall area

DIRECTIONS

1. For wall pushups, instruct the child to stand at arm's length from the wall (first image).

2. Have them slowly move their body toward the wall without moving their hands or feet (second image).

3. Repeat 5 to 10 repetitions.

4. For wall sits, have them sit against the wall without moving their feet (third image).

5. Have the child hold the position for 15 to 30 seconds. Repeat three times.

 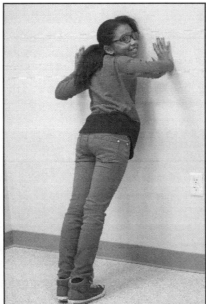 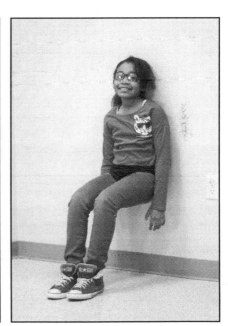

ROLLING LIKE A BALL

AIM To allow the opportunity for movement to increase attention and decrease primitive reflex activation (e.g., Tonic Labyrinthine reflex)

YOU WILL NEED

- An open floor area

DIRECTIONS

1. Have the child hold their legs close to their chest.

2. Ask them to roll back, then forward, and repeat.

3. Have the child attempt to perform 5 to 10 repetitions.

THE SNAKE

AIM To allow the opportunity for movement to increase attention and decrease primitive reflex activation (e.g., Landau reflex)

YOU WILL NEED

- An open floor area

DIRECTIONS

1. Have the child lie on their belly.

2. Ask them to press their upper body up with straight arms and legs.

3. Encourage them not to move their legs.

4. Have them hold the position, while breathing, for about 10 seconds and then lower their upper body to the floor.

5. Have the child perform 5 to 10 repetitions.

THE TABLE

AIM To allow the opportunity for movement to increase core strength and decrease primitive reflex activation

YOU WILL NEED

- An open floor area

DIRECTIONS

1. Have the child sit on the floor.

2. Ask them to place their arms behind them and raise their bottom off of the floor.

3. Have them hold the position, while breathing, for about 10 seconds and then lower their bottom to the floor.

4. Have the child perform 5 to 10 repetitions.

SUN BATHING

AIM To allow opportunity for movement to increase attention and decrease primitive reflex activation (e.g., Moro reflex)

YOU WILL NEED

- An open area

DIRECTIONS

1. Have the child stand with straight legs.

2. Ask them to place their arms above their head and look up, as in the following image. (Optional: Have them stand on one leg.)

3. Have them hold the position, while breathing, for about 10 seconds and then lower their arms.

4. Have the child perform 5 to 10 repetitions.

SNOW ANGEL

AIM To allow the opportunity for movement to increase attention and decrease primitive reflex activation (e.g., Moro reflex)

YOU WILL NEED

- An open floor area

DIRECTIONS

1. Have the child lie on the floor.

2. Ask them to place their arms at their sides with straight legs.

3. Have them open their arms and legs like they were making an angel in the snow.

4. Have them hold the open position, while breathing, for about 10 seconds before moving to the closed position.

5. Have the child perform 5 to 10 repetitions.

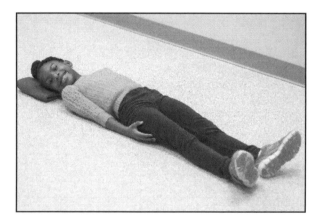

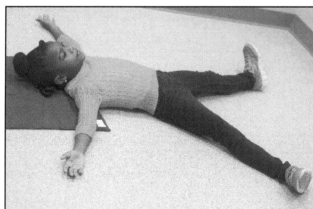

HORSE AND CAMEL

AIM To allow the opportunity for movement to increase attention and decrease primitive reflex activation (e.g., Symmetrical Tonic Neck and Galant reflexes)

YOU WILL NEED

- An open floor area

DIRECTIONS

1. Have the child get on all fours.

2. Have them flatten their back like a horse.

3. Next, ask them to round their back like a camel, as in the following image.

4. Have them hold the horse position, while breathing, for about 10 seconds before moving to the camel position.

5. Have the child perform 5 to 10 repetitions.

WALL POSES

AIM To allow the opportunity for movement to increase attention and decrease primitive reflex activation (e.g., ATNR)

YOU WILL NEED

- An open wall area

DIRECTIONS

1. Have the child stand sideways next to the wall.

2. Ask them to extend their arm closest to the wall and place their hand on the wall.

3. On the opposite side, have them place their hand on their hip and look over their shoulder, as in the following image.

4. Have the child turn around and repeat on the other side.

5. Have them hold each position, while breathing, for about 10 seconds before moving to the next position.

6. Have the child perform 5 to 10 repetitions.

chapter 16

Inhibition Activities

In this chapter activities are focused on exercising inhibition and assist in identifying the ninth daily target.

At the beginning of each of the following activities, the activity level is identified according to the **Self-Regulation and Mindfulness 7-Level Hierarchy.** As you may recall, Levels 1 through 4 on the hierarchy correspond with higher-level activities, Level 5 corresponds with midlevel activities, and Levels 6 and 7 correspond with foundational-level activities. The Threshold and Arousal Levels Table in Chapter 4 can be used to identify the child's levels. Be sure to keep track of which activities work for the child and their reactions to the activities.

General strategies:

- "Red light, green light" and "freeze tag" are great games that involve inhibition.
- Staring contests and "who can be quiet the longest" also challenge this ability.
- Remember to use multisensory stimuli! Use metronomes, change the lighting, or turn on music.

THE VACATION GAME

AIM To decrease sensory-seeking, avoiding, and inattentive behaviors and provide an organizing activity to enhance appropriate attention levels

Suggested Starting Hierarchy Level Midlevel to high on page ix

Appropriate Arousal Level All arousal levels*

Appropriate Threshold Level All thresholds*

YOU WILL NEED

- Polyvinyl placement markers or rug squares
- Music

DIRECTIONS

1. Have each child stand on a spot (designated by a placement marker or rug square; placement markers made of tape can be used as well). The spot is the child's "vacation island."

2. Play music and have the children walk, crab walk, or crawl to a new island. Have them move in a circular fashion around the spots for synchrony, or they can move randomly among the spots.

3. Stop the music. Each child should land on a new spot.

4. Encourage them to share what new views they see on their new "island."

5. Pretend the temperature has changed: If it is hot, ask them to "melt" to the ground. If it is cold, have them stand up and "freeze."

6. Pretend the "vacation" has moved to outer space.

7. Play the music again, and have the children move until they land on a new spot when the music stops.

8. Have them "moon dance" in slow motion to the music on their new "outer space" location.

*The threshold indicates how easily the child detects stimuli, or changes in their environment (low = quick detection; high = slow detection). A child's arousal is the behavioral reaction to stimuli that we can observe.

START STOP

AIM To decrease sensory avoiding and inattentive behaviors and provide an organizing activity to enhance appropriate attention levels

Suggested Starting Hierarchy Level Foundational on page ix

Appropriate Arousal Level High (overreaction) or low (lack of response)*

Appropriate Threshold Level High (hypervigilant) or (inattentive)*

YOU WILL NEED

- An open area

DIRECTIONS

1. Instruct the child to engage in at least three movements, such as clapping, marching in place, and waving their arms by the sides.

2. Connect each movement with a command (e.g., "go," "slow," "stop") or color: "When I say 'green,' you clap; when I say 'red,' you march; when I say 'yellow,' wave your arms by your sides."

3. Start the activity and ensure that the child changes their movements throughout.

4. To provide an additional challenge, change up the word that corresponds with each movement: "Now 'red' means clap."

*The threshold indicates how easily the child detects stimuli, or changes in their environment (low = quick detection; high = slow detection). A child's arousal is the behavioral reaction to stimuli that we can observe.

SPIN TOP

AIM To decrease sensory-seeking and inattentive behaviors and provide an organizing activity to enhance appropriate attention levels

Suggested Starting Hierarchy Level Foundational on page ix

Appropriate Arousal Level High (energetic) or low (lack of response)*

Appropriate Threshold Level High (hyperactive) or (inattentive)*

YOU WILL NEED

- An open space
- A rotating chair, stool, or swing

DIRECTIONS

1. Place the child on the chair, stool, or swing.

2. Spin them to the right, then stop and freeze. Swing them to the left, then stop and freeze.

3. Repeat five times on each side.

4. Follow with deep pressure, such as giving big hugs or have the child lie under a bean bag chair.

*The threshold indicates how easily the child detects stimuli, or changes in their environment (low = quick detection; high = slow detection). A child's arousal is the behavioral reaction to stimuli that we can observe.

SWINGING, CRASHING, OR PULLING

AIM To decrease sensory avoiding and inattentive behaviors and provide an organizing activity to enhance appropriate attention levels

Suggested Starting Hierarchy Level Foundational on page ix

Appropriate Arousal Level High (energetic) or low (lack of response)*

Appropriate Threshold Level High (hyperactive) or (inattentive)*

Note With the guidance of a professional, hypervigilant children can benefit from this activity as well.

YOU WILL NEED

- A body sock
- Open space

DIRECTIONS

1. Place the child inside the body sock.

2. Pull them across a smooth surface.

3. You may also safely lift and crash them onto a soft surface, such as a mattress or crash pad.

4. For small children, two adults can lift and swing the child between them.

5. Be sure to pause for at least 3 to 5 seconds between repetitions. Ask the child to request more to encourage engagement.

*The threshold indicates how easily the child detects stimuli, or changes in their environment
(low = quick detection; high = slow detection). A child's arousal is the behavioral reaction to stimuli that we can observe.

chapter 17

Troubleshooting Challenging Behaviors

Every child is different. Use your judgment and expertise to make knowledgeable decisions. Remember, parents are the experts on their own child. We must work together for optimal success and the child's best quality of life. Pull from the concepts in this program as you desire. Although I encourage you to attempt to address all of the underlying principles, this should not be a strictly prescribed program. You should seek opportunities to incorporate the targets in everyday tasks.

Now, let us troubleshoot some challenging behaviors. We start with difficulty sleeping and eating, followed by self-injurious and risky behaviors.

Following are some ideas to improve sleep hygiene.

1. Every person has a "sweet spot" of timing for optimal sleep. Our bodies naturally release melatonin. Melatonin does not put us to sleep—it prepares our body for rest by causing it to slow down the amount of stimulation it receives. Sleep is optimal 30 minutes after melatonin is released.

   Have you ever heard of someone saying that a baby is overtired? Well, that means that the baby's body released melatonin, but the environment is not supporting the body's attempt to rest, resulting in an internal conflict that leads to overactivation of the RAS. The baby becomes aroused and starts receiving a lot of sensory information. When the baby is later put down for sleep, it is too late: They are now cranky, and their body is uncomfortable.

2. Try identifying the "sweet spot" when melatonin is released. This requires "backward chaining" (working backward from the goal). Try allowing the child to stay awake a little later than you desire. Observe and see when they appear to get tired. You may initially observe an increase of energy followed by a slow-down phase. They may rub their eyes or yawn. At that moment, attempt to place them in bed or ask them to lie down. This may happen very late, past the ideal bedtime.

   If trying to put a child to bed at your desired time leads to worse sleeping patterns, you may need to compromise. Identify that optimal time, and try putting the child to bed at that time for a few days using a bedtime routine (e.g., bath time, deep pressure massage, then calming aromatherapy). Then, attempt to start your routine an hour earlier every few days to a week. You may want to talk about the use of melatonin supplements for additional support.

3. Our bodies naturally respond to certain positions. When our arms and legs are extended away from our bodies, we are alert and allow sensory information to enter our bodies. When our arms and legs are flexed toward our bodies, we allow less stimulation to come into our sensory system. The RAS, along with another brain structure called the cerebellum, responds to these positions. In addition, when your feet leave the ground, the RAS and cerebellum communicate to prepare the body for rest. For children with extremely poor sleep habits, you may want to explore using a hammock swing or hammock bed. Rocking is another technique that often works.

4. Ear and scalp massage may be helpful. Slow, rhythmic, gentle stroking and massaging of the scalp and ears may slow down brain waves and signal the body to rest. Nerves in the external ear connect to the vagus nerve. If you recall, the vagus nerve is also connected to our system for rest and digestion. The vagus nerve is very powerful: Stimulation can lead to decreased arousal. Slow rhythmic strokes over the scalp are very relaxing. Be sure to use your fingertips only. Children will sometimes bang their head in an attempt to slow down their brain waves for rest. Scalp and ear massage may act as a safer replacement for head banging.

Following are some ideas for addressing difficulty eating.

1. Allow the child time to explore food without eating. Let them use their hands to play and sculpt figures with pureed food. Encourage them to be silly and smear food on the table then on their hands, then arms, and then face.

2. Present food from in front of the child. Do not try to trick them. They are very aware of unwanted stimuli! Sit in front of them and start by showing the food before placing it into their mouth.

3. Stimulate the hands and mouth with vibration, which may desensitize the area. If possible, combine vibration with ice (e.g., use a vibrating frozen teething device). Our body naturally decreases the pain and tactile responses when cold and vibration are presented.

4. Sometimes, hypersensitivity to sound (e.g., chewing) can cause challenges with eating. Try addressing the child's auditory system. If the child wears headphones with preferred music at a high volume (remaining safe for their ears) while eating, they may not be bothered by the sound of their chewing.

Following are some ideas for addressing self-injurious behaviors.

1. Children who self-injure typically have a high threshold. Ice therapy should be attempted. Remember that pain and temperature are neurologically connected. Review the target activities for ideas. When using ice therapy, allow the child time to hold, manipulate, and even eat ice chips. You want to meet their high threshold.

2. Try to identify the trigger. Is the child presenting such behaviors without any catalyst? For example, are they banging their head during independent play? Perhaps they are in need of a sensory approach. Weighted caps, head wraps, and deep-pressure massage may be warranted. If they are biting their hands, you may want to try tight-fitting or weighted gloves, such as boxing gloves. Pressure and weighted vests can be used as well.

    If you do notice a trigger, such as your asking the child to do work, try changing the routine. Perhaps a change of environment or having the child perform a task at a different time of day can help. If there is an object that triggers the response, such as a plate during mealtime or a book during class, try to change the object; for example, use a different plate or copy pages from the book and present single pages.

Following are some ideas for addressing risky behaviors.

1. Some children are risk takers. Remember that the IC teaches us what is right and what is wrong. In working with children who like to take risks, start with the SAM practices in an attempt to slow down the seeking parts of the brain. When we meditate or perform other activities that connect the mind and body, our IC gets stronger. Be sure to have the child do deep belly breathing, as that has an impact on the IC.

2. Try to incorporate intense activities to meet the child's threshold. Avoid offering short bursts of vestibular activities, such as bouncing on a trampoline, swinging, or freeze dance, which enhance the child's arousal without meeting their needs or threshold. This may only make things worse. Try more controlled movement breaks with heavy work and weights. You must combine the activities with stimulation of multiple sensory areas. For example, if the child is swinging, use a blindfold, turn up the music, and push them intensely. Seek out a sensory gym to allow for climbing and crashing. Rock climbing and swimming are great activities.

Appendix
Fun Projects
& Songs

How to Make a Homemade Snow Globe

Playing with snow globes is a great visual and mindful activity.

YOU WILL NEED

- A clear plastic bottle
- Glitter
- A small toy or other object (optional)
- A pipe cleaner (optional)
- Waterproof glue (optional)

DIRECTIONS

1. Obtain a bottle, such as a disposable water bottle.

2. Place glitter in the bottle.

3. Fill it with water.

4. To be more creative, glue a small toy or other object to a pipe cleaner and attach the end of the pipe cleaner to the inside of the lid so the object extends into the bottle.

5. Use the bottle for SAM Breaks or place it in the SAM Box.

HOW TO MAKE A FIDGET

Fidgets are great to keep the hands busy during class or other times when sitting is required.

YOU WILL NEED

- A balloon
- A funnel
- Water beads

DIRECTIONS

1. You can use a funnel to place the water beads inside the balloon.

2. Pour a small amount of water in the balloon as indicated in the directions for the water beads.

3. Watch the balloon fidget expand.

4. Be sure to secure the end of the balloon.

5. This may not be an appropriate object for younger children or those frequently mouthing objects.

6. You can freeze the fidget to increase the intensity of stimulation it provides.

HOW TO MAKE SENSORY SANDBAGS

These are great for carrying in the hallways at school!

YOU WILL NEED

- An empty gallon-size milk or detergent bottle or a small drawstring backpack
- Fish gravel

DIRECTIONS

1. Fill the milk bottle, detergent bottle, or backpack with the fish gravel at a level that is safe for the child to carry (no more than 10% of their body weight).

2. Identify opportunities for the child to carry the object, such as during transitions between class or on SAM Breaks.

HOW TO MAKE EYE SANDBAGS

Pressure on the eyes triggers a natural parasympathetic response.

YOU WILL NEED

- Two clean white tube socks
- Aquarium gravel
- Markers or paint

DIRECTIONS

1. Take one sock and allow the child to decorate it with the markers or paint.

2. Encourage them to make eyes on one side.

3. Fill the other sock with the gravel.

4. Secure the end by knotting or sewing.

5. Place it into the decorated sock, with the sewn or knotted side going in first.

6. Secure the decorated sock by sewing or knotting.

7. The child can lay the sandbag over their eyes during brain breaks, before bed, or during sensory activities such as swinging.

HOW TO MAKE A SMELL SACK

Do not forget about the sense of smell. Smells can help to calm or alert the child.

YOU WILL NEED

- A small organza bag
- Essential oils (lavender and wood smells to calm, citrus smells to alert)
- Dry rice
- Coffee beans

DIRECTIONS

1. Place the dry rice inside the organza bag.

2. Sprinkle a few drops of the essential oils inside.

3. Be selective with the scents you choose based on the child's arousal level and threshold.

4. You can use multiple bags to explore the child's preferences.

5. Have the child smell coffee beans in between smelling the various oil-scented bags.

Songs for the Senses and Feelings

These Are Our Senses

(To the tune of "Where is Thumbkin")
These are my senses, These are my senses
My body, My body
Love my senses, Love my senses
Every day, Every day

These are my eyes (repeat)
Help me see (repeat)
Love my eyes (repeat)
Every day (repeat)

These are my ears (repeat)
Help me hear (repeat)
Love my ears (repeat)
Every day (repeat)

These are my muscles (repeat)
Help me move (repeat)
Love my muscles (repeat)
Every day (repeat)

This is my skin (repeat)
Helps me touch (repeat)
Love my skin (repeat)
Every day (repeat)

This is my tongue (repeat)
Helps me taste (repeat)
Love my tongue (repeat)
Every day (repeat)

This is my nose (repeat)
Helps me smell (repeat)
Love my nose (repeat)
Every day (repeat)

This is my head (repeat)
Helps me think (repeat)
Love my head (repeat)
Every day (repeat)

Feelings Song

(To the tune of "The Alphabet Song")
I have feelings, what about you?
What are feelings, what do they do?
Some are FADS, and some are JELs
They make you sad, or make you glad
But we know just what to do
Don't let your feelings take over you
Remember to stop and then to think
Blow out the feelings, then take a long blink

References

Alvarado, J. C., Vaughan, J. W., Stanford, T. R., & Stein, B. E. (2007). Multisensory versus unisensory integration: Contrasting modes in the superior colliculus. *Journal of Neurophysiology, 97*(5), 3193–3205.

American Psychiatric Association (2013). *Diagnostic and statistical manual of mental disorders,* 5th ed. Arlington, VA: American Psychiatric Association Publishing.

Augustine, J. R. (1996). Circuitry and functional aspects of the insular lobe in primates, including humans. *Brain Research Reviews, 22*(3), 229–244.

Ayres, A. J. (1963). The 1963 Eleanor Clarke Slagle lecture—The development of perceptual–motor abilities: A theoretical basis for treatment of dysfunction. *American Journal of Occupational Therapy, 17* (6), 127–135.

Ayres, A. J. (1965). Patterns of perceptual–motor dysfunction in children: A factor analytic study. *Perceptual and Motor Skills, 20,* 335–368.

Ayres, A. J. (1972). Sensory integration and learning disorders. Los Angeles: Western Psychological Services.

Ayres, A. J. (1979). Sensory integration and the child. Los Angeles: Western Psychological Services.

Badre, D., & Wagner, A. D. (2002). Semantic retrieval, mnemonic control, and prefrontal cortex. *Behavioral and Cognitive Neuroscience Reviews, 1*(3), 206–218.

Bandura, A. (1991). Social cognitive theory of self-regulation. *Organizational Behavior and Human Decision Processes, 50*(2), 248–287.

Ben-Sasson, A., Carter, A. S., & Briggs-Gowan, M. J. (2009). *Journal of Abnormal Child Pscholology, 37,* 705. doi:10.1007/s10802-008-9295-8

Biegel, G. M., Brown, K. W., Shapiro, S. L., & Schubert, C. M. (2009). Mindfulness-based stress reduction for the treatment of adolescent psychiatric outpatients: A randomized clinical trial. *Journal of Consulting and Clinical Psychology. 77*(5), 855–866. doi: 0022-006X/09/$12.00 doi: 10.1037/a0016241

Chaidez, V., Hansen, R. L., & Hertz-Picciotto, I. (2015). Gastrointestinal problems in children with autism: Developmental delays or typical development. *Journal of Autism and Developmental Disorders, 44,* 1117–1127.

Chung, W. (March, 2014). Wendy Chung: Autism—What we know (and what we don't know yet) [Video file]. Retrieved from https://www.ted.com/talks/wendy_chung_autism_what_we_know_and_what_we_don_t_know_yet

Fried, M., Tsitsiashvili, E., Bonneh, Y. S., Sterkin, A., Wygnanski-Jaffe, T., Epstein, T., Polat, U. (2014). ADHD subjects fail to suppress eye blinks and microsaccades while anticipating visual stimuli but recover with medication. *Vision Research, 101,* 62–72.

Gogolla, N., Takesian, A. E., Feng, G., Fagiolini, M., & Hensch, T. K. (2014). Sensory integration in mouse insular cortex reflects GABA circuit maturation. *Neuron, 83*(4), 894-905.

Hermans, E. J., van Marle, H. J., Ossewaarde, L., Henckens, M. J., van Kesteren, M. T., Schoots, V. C., Cousijn, H., Rijpkema, M., Oostenveld, R., & Fernández, G. (2011). Stress-related noradrenergic activity prompts large-scale neural network reconfiguration. *Science, 334*(6059), 1151–1153. doi: 10.1126/science.1209603

Holland, K., & Higuera, V. (2015). The history of ADHD: A timeline written by Kimberly Holland and Valencia Higuera Retrieved from http://www.healthline.com/health/adhd/history#Overview1

Hsiao, E. Y., McBride, S. W., Hsien, S., Sharon, G., Hyde, E. R., McCue, T., Codelli, J. A., Chow, J., Reisman, S. E., Petrosino, J. F., Patterson, P. H., & Mazmanian, S. K. (2013). Microbiota modulate behavioral and physiological abnormalities associated with neurodevelopmental disorders. *Cell, 155*(7), 1451–1463.

Kabat-Zinn, J. (1994). Wherever you go, there you are: Mindfulness meditation in everyday life. New York: Hachette Books.

Kanner, L. (1943). Autistic disturbances of affective contact. *Nervous Child, 2,* 217–250.

Kelly, C., Toro, R., Di Martino, A., & Milham, M. P. (2012). A convergent functional architecture of the insula emerges across imaging modalities. *NeuroImage. 61*(4), 1129–1142. doi: 10.106/j.neuroimage.2012.03.021

Konicarova, J., & Bob, P. (2013). Principle of dissolution and primitive reflexes in ADHD. *Activitas Nervosa Superior, 55*(1/2), 74.

Kurth, F., Zilles, K., Fox, P. T., Laird, A. R., & Eickhoff, S. B. (2010). A link between the systems: Functional differentiation and integration within the human insula revealed by meta-analysis. *Brain Structure and Function, 214,* 519-534. doi 10.1007/s00429-010-0255-z

Larson, P. D. & Stensaas, S. S. (2005). PediNeurologic exam: A neurodevelopmental approach [Video]. Retrieved from http://library.med.utah.edu/pedineurologicexam/html/home_exam.html

LeDoux, J. (1998). The Emotional brain: The mysterious underpinnings of emotional life. New York: Simon & Schuster.

Maslow, A. H. (1943). A theory of human motivation. *Psychological Review,* 50 (4): 370–96. doi:10.1037/h0054346

Maslow, A. H. (1970). *Religions, values, and peak experiences.* New York: Penguin. (Original work published 1964).

Mazurek, M. O., Vasa, R. A., Kalb, L. G., Kanne, S. M., Rosenberg, D., Keefer, A., Murray D. S., Freedman, B., & Lowery, L. A. (2013). Anxiety, sensory over-responsivity, and gastrointestinal problems in children with autism spectrum disorders. *Journal of Abnormal Child Psycholology, 41,* 165–176.

McElhanon, B. O., McCracken, C., Karpen, S., & Sharp, W. G. (2014). Gastrointestinal symptoms in Autism Spectrum Disorder: A meta-analysis. *Pediatrics, 33,* 872–883.

McFarlane, H. G., Kusek, G. K., Yang, M., Phoenix, J. L., Bolivar, V. J., *&* Crawley, J. N. (2008). Autism-like behavioral phenotypes in BTBR T+tf/J mice. *Genes, Brain, and Behavior, 7*(2):152–163.

Menon, V., & Uddin, L. Q. (2010). Saliency, switching, attention and control: a network model of insula function. *Brain Structure and Function, 214,* 655–667. doi: 10.1007/s00429-010-0262-0

Miller, L. J., Anzalone, M. E., Lane, S. J., Cermak, S. A., & Osten, E. T. (2007). Concept evolution in sensory integration: A proposed nosology for diagnosis. *American Journal of Occupational Therapy, 61*(2), 135–140. doi: 10.5014/ajot.61.2.135.

Miller, L. J., & Schaaf, R. C. (2008). Sensory Processing Disorder. *Encyclopedia of Infant and Early Childhood Development,* 127-136, doi:10.1016/b978-012370877-9.00142-0

Napoli, M., Krech, P. R., Holley, L. C. (2009). Mindfulness training for elementary school students: The attention academy. *Journal of Applied School Psychology, 21,* 99–125.

Nieuwenhuys, R. (2012). The insular cortex: A review. *Progress in Brain Research, 195,* 123–163. doi: 10.1016/B978-0-444-53860-4.00007-6Pearson, B. L., Pobbe, R. L., Defensor, E. B., Oasay, L., Bolivar, V. J., Blanchard, D. C., & Blanchard, R. J. (2011). Motor and cognitive stereotypies in the BTBR T+tf/J mouse model of autism. *Genes, Brain, and Behavior, 10,* 228–235.

Reflexes explained. (2005). *Retained Neonatal Reflexes.* Retrieved from http://www.retainedneonatalreflexes.com.au/reflexes-explained/

Seymour, B., Daw, N., Dayan, P., Singer, T., & *Dolan,* R. (2007). Differential encoding of losses and gains in the human striatum. *Journal of Neuroscience, 27*(18), 4826–4831. doi: https://doi.org/10.1523/JNEUROSCI.0400-07.2007

Stein, B. E., & Meredith, M. A. (1993). *The merging of the senses.* Cambridge, MA: The MIT Press.

Taylor, M., Houghton, S., & Chapman, E. (2005). Primitive reflexes and attention-deficit/hyperactivity disorder: Developmental origins of classroom dysfunction. *International Journal of Special Education, 19(1),* 23–37.

Uddin, L. Q., & Menon, V. (2009). The anterior insula in autism: under-connected and under-examined. *Neuroscience & Biobehavioral Reviews, 33*(8), 1198-1203.

Wing, L., & Gould, J. (1979). Severe impairments of social interaction and associated abnormalities in children: Epidemiology and classification. *Journal of Autism and Developmental Disorders, 9*(1), 11–29.

Wylie, K. P., & Tregellas, J. R. (2010). The role of the insula in schizophrenia. *Schizophrenia Research, 123*(2–3), 93–104. doi: 10.1016/j.schres.2010.08.027

Glossary

Arousal: One's level of wakefulness, attentiveness, and activity

Behavior: An observable physical response to sensory integration, or a change in our feelings

Emotional Regulation: Our ability to control or adapt to our internal and external reactions to a feeling following an experience/event

Executive Functioning: Abilities that include an individual's problem-solving skills, attention, flexibility, inhibitory control, and reasoning

Inhibitory Control: The ability to cease emotional reactions to produce an appropriate response

Interoception: The internal detection of changes in one's internal organs through specific sensory receptors

Mindfulness: "Being a witness to one's own personal experience" through awareness of all sensations and emotions in the present moment

Multisensory Integration: Neurological synchrony of sensory systems processing stimuli simultaneously

Praxis: Having an idea, planning it out, and executing it, which entails the motor output involved in various activities, including organization of required tasks

Proprioception: The sensory system located in joints and muscles that allows for awareness of where one's body is in space

Reaction: An observable emotional response lacking cognitive processing

Reciprocal Regulation: The interaction of two or more individuals resulting in change of arousal and overall self-regulation of those involved

Response: An observable action produced following appraisal of emotions through engagement of executive functioning

Self-Regulation: One's awareness and ability to control and adapt multisensory integration, emotional regulation, and executive functioning for functional interaction with the environment and others

Sensory Integration: Theory used to describe one's ability to take in two or more sensory stimuli to produce a functional and meaningful response

Sensory Processing Disorder (SPD): Dysfunction in sensory modulation, discrimination, and sensorimotor activity manifesting as difficulty with social-emotional interaction and self-regulation

Sensory Stimulation: The detection of changes in the environment or internally through one's sensory receptors

Sensory Stimulus: The object or event leading to detection of change in a person's sensory system

Threshold: How quickly and easily a person reacts to a sensory stimulus

Vestibular: The sensory system located in the inner ear that allows one to detect the head moving through space, providing a sense of balance and spatial orientation